PROJECT
SUCCESS 1

Betsy Wong
MaryAnn Florez

Series Consultants
Susan Gaer
Sarah Lynn

The publisher would like to thank Irene Frankel for her creative conception and vision for this groundbreaking course.

PROJECT SUCCESS 1

Pearson Education, 10 Bank Street, White Plains, NY 10606

Staff Credits: The people who made up the *Project Success* team, representing editorial, production, design, and manufacturing, are Peter Benson, Andrea Bryant, Maretta Callahan, Iris Candelaria, Aerin Csigay, Mindy DePalma, Dave Dickey, Christine Edmonds, Nancy Flaggman, Ann France, Aliza Greenblatt, Gosia Jaros-White, Caroline Kasterine, Amy Kefauver, Niki Lee, Jaime Lieber, Jessica Miller-Smith, Tracey Munz Cataldo, Laurie Neaman, Jenn Raspiller, Julie Schmidt, Kim Snyder, Katherine Sullivan, Loretta Steeves, Jane Townsend, Ken Volcjak, and Martin Yu.

Interior Design: Word & Image

Cover Design: Ann France and Tracey Munz Cataldo

Text Composition: TSI Graphics

Text font: Franklin Gothic

For photo and illustration credits, please turn to the back of the book.

Library of Congress Cataloging-in-Publication Data
Lynn, Sarah.
  Project success : skills for the 21st century / Sarah Lynn ; Series Consultants: Susan Gaer, Sarah Lynn.
      pages cm
  Summary: Project Success is a blended-learning digital and print course with a strong focus on workplace skills, career readiness, and 21st century challenges. This unique video-based series engages learners with high-interest video vignettes that represent a "day in the life" of characters in diverse workplace settings that may simulate their own. Integrated skills lessons encourage critical thinking and problem solving woven into the students' English language learning journey.
   ISBN 978-0-13-294236-2 — ISBN 978-0-13-248297-4 — ISBN 978-0-13-294238-6 —
   ISBN 978-0-13-294240-9 — ISBN 978-0-13-294242-3 — ISBN 978-0-13-298513-0
   1. English language—Textbooks for foreign speakers. 2. English language—Spoken English. 3. English language—Sound recordings for foreign speakers. 4. English language—Study and teaching—Foreign speakers—Audio-visual aids. 5. Business communication—United States—Vocational guidance. I. Gaer, Susan. II. Title.
   PE1128.L98 2014
   428.2'4—dc23

2013035851

ISBN-10: 0-13-248297-5
ISBN-13: 978-0-13-248297-4

Printed in the United States of America
2 17

Contents

Acknowledgments iv

About the Series Consultants and Authors v

Scope and Sequence.. vi–ix

To the Teacher.. x

To the Student 1

WELCOME UNIT 2

UNIT 1 **Truda's New Job**.................................... 5

UNIT 2 **Carmen's Busy Day** 19

UNIT 3 **Oscar Is in Charge** 33

UNIT 4 **Wen Likes his Job** 47

UNIT 5 **Saba Doesn't Feel Well** 61

UNIT 6 **Saba Goes to the Doctor**...................... 75

UNIT 7 **Oscar Wants to Move**............................ 89

UNIT 8 **Wen's Surprise**................................... 103

UNIT 9 **Truda Asks for Help**............................ 117

UNIT 10 **Carmen Gets an Invitation**.................. 131

Grammar Review 145

Grammar References... 155

Word List.. 156

Job Application... 161

Maps 162

Acknowledgments

The authors and publisher would like to offer sincere thanks to our Series Consultants for lending their expertise and insights and for helping shape the course.

Susan Gaer Santa Ana College School of Continuing Education, Santa Ana, CA

Sarah Lynn Harvard Bridge to Learning and Literacy Program, Cambridge, MA

In addition, we would like to express gratitude to the following people. Their kind participation was invaluable to the creation of this program.

Consultants

Robert Breitbard, Director of Adult & Community Education, Collier County Public Schools, Naples, Florida; **Ingrid Greenberg**, Associate Professor, ESL, and Past-President, Academic Senate, Continuing Education, San Diego Community College District, San Diego, California; **Vittoria G. Maghsoudi-Abbate**, Assistant Director, Mt. Diablo Adult Education, Mt. Diablo USD, Concord, California; **Irina Patten**, Lone Star College-Fairbanks Center, Houston, Texas; **Maria Soto Caratini**, Eastfield College DCCCD, Mesquite, Texas; **Claire Valier**, Palm Beach County, Florida; **Jacqueline S. Walpole**, Director, Adult Education, Prince George's Community College, Largo, Maryland.

Reviewers

Eleanor Brockman-Forfang, Instructor, Special Projects (ESL), Tarrant County College, South Campus, Fort Worth, TX; **Natalya Dollar**, ESL Program Resource Coordinator, North Orange County Community College District, Anaheim, CA; **Bette Empol**, ESL, ABE, GED Prep and Bridge Coordinator, Conejo Valley Adult School, Thousand Oaks, CA; **Mark Fisher**, Lone Star College-Fairbanks Center, Houston, TX; **Ann Fontanella**, ESL Instructor, City College of San Francisco, San Francisco, CA; **Ingrid Greenberg**, Associate Professor, ESL, and Past-President, Academic Senate, Continuing Education, San Diego Community College District, San Diego, CA; **Janet Harclerode**, Santa Monica College, Santa Monica, CA; **Laura Jensen**, ESL Instructor, North Seattle Community College, Seattle, WA; **Tommie Martinez**, Fresno Adult School, Fresno, CA; **Suzanne L. Monti**, ESOL Instructional Specialist, Community College of Baltimore County, Continuing Education, Baltimore, MD; **Kelly Nusz**, Carlos Rosario Charter School, Washington, D.C; **Irina Patten**, Lone Star College-Fairbanks Center, Houston, TX; **Ariel Peckokas**, Collier County Public Schools Adult Education, Naples, FL; **Sydney Rice**, Imperial Valley College, Imperial, CA; **Richard Salvador**, McKinley Community Schools of Arts, Honolulu, Hawaii; **Maria Soto Caratini**, Eastfield College DCCCD, Mesquite, TX; **Patty Swartzbaugh**, Nashville Adult Literacy Council, Nashville, TN; **Candace Thompson-Lynch**, ESL Instructor, School of Continuing Education, North Orange County Community College District, Anaheim, CA; **Esther M. Tillet**, Miami Dade College-Wolfson Campus, Miami, FL; **Adriana Treadway**, Assistant Director, Spring International Language Center, University of Arkansas, Fayetteville, AR; **Monica C. Vazquez**, ESOL Adjunct Instructor, Brookhaven College, DCCCD, Farmers Branch, TX.

Thanks also to the teachers who contributed their valuable ideas for the Persistence Activities: **Dave Coleman** Los Angeles Unified School District, Los Angeles, CA; **Renee Collins** Elk Grove Adult and Community Education, Elk Grove, CA; **Elaine Klapman** Venice Community Adult School, Venice, CA (retired); **Yvonne Wong Nishio** Evans Community Adult School, Los Angeles, CA; **Daniel S. Pittaway** North Orange County Community College District, Anaheim, CA; **Laurel Pollard** Educational Consultant, Tucson, AZ; **Eden Quimzon** Santiago Canyon College, Division of Continuing Education, Orange, CA.

Special thanks to **Ronna Magy** for her invaluable contributions to the Job-Seeking Skills lessons and to **Sharon Goldstein** for her skilled writing of the pronunciation strand.

SERIES CONSULTANTS

Susan Gaer has worked as an ESL teacher since 1980 and currently teaches at the Santa Ana College School of Continuing Education. She is an avid user of technology and trains teachers online for TESOL and the Outreach Technical Assistance Center (OTAN). Susan is a frequent presenter at local, state, national, and international conferences on using the latest technology with adult learners from the literacy level through transition to college. She has co-authored books and teacher's manuals, served on the executive boards for CATESOL (California Teachers of English to Speakers of Other Languages) and TESOL, and contributed to standing committees for professional development and technology. Susan holds a master's degree in English with emphasis in TESOL from San Francisco State University and a master's degree in Educational Technology from Pepperdine University.

Sarah Lynn has over twenty-five years of teaching experience in ESOL. She has dedicated much of her teaching life to working with low-level learners with interrupted education. Currently she teaches at the Harvard Bridge Program, Harvard University. As a teacher trainer, Sarah has led professional development workshops throughout the United States on topics such as teaching in the multilevel classroom, learner persistence, twenty-first-century skills, self-directed learning, collaborative learning, and scaffolding learning for the literacy learner. As a consultant, she has written ESOL curricula for programs in civics, literacy, phonics, and English language arts. As a materials writer, she has contributed to numerous Pearson ELT publications, including *Business Across Cultures, Future, Future U.S. Citizens*, and *Project Success*. Sarah holds a master's degree in TESOL from Teacher's College, Columbia University.

AUTHORS

Betsy Lindeman Wong has worked in adult ESL for nearly 20 years as an instructor, site coordinator, curriculum developer, and trainer. Currently an instructor in Northern Virginia Community College's American Culture and Language Institute, she has taught ESL in academic and workplace settings as well as in community education and family literacy programs. She has also taught English as a Foreign Language in France. She holds a master's degree in French and a graduate certificate in TESOL from American University. The coauthor of Pearson Longman's *Future English for Results 5: Teacher's Edition and Lesson Planner*, she regularly presents workshops on ESL literacy, multilevel strategies, lifeskill instruction, and communicative language techniques.

MaryAnn Cunningham Florez is the Program Manager for Fairfax County, Virginia's Public School Adult ESOL Program, where she coordinates classes that draw more than 6,000 enrollments per year. Previously, MaryAnn was the Director of the Adult Education Professional Development Center of D.C. Learns, overseeing professional development for the District of Columbia's ABE, GED, and adult ESOL educators. She also has served as the Lead ESL Specialist at the Arlington Educational and Employment Program (REEP), as Assistant Director of the National Center for ESL Literacy Education at the Center for Applied Linguistics, and as chair of TESOL's Adult Education Interest Section. She holds a master's degree in adult education from George Mason University. MaryAnn has been an author and a series consultant on various adult ESOL materials and textbooks published by New Readers Press and by Pearson, and she is codeveloper of a series of teacher training DVDs produced by the New American Horizons Foundation.

Scope and Sequence 1

Unit	Listening/Speaking VIDEO	Grammar VIDEO	Practical Skills	Pronunciation	Reading Skills
Welcome page 2	• Introduce yourself • Say where you are from • Follow classroom instructions • Ask for repetition	• (embedded: Subject pronouns: *I, you, he, she, it, we, they*)	• Read and fill out a student identification card	NA	• Learn about your book
1 **Truda's New Job** page 5	• Introduce yourself • Say what you do • Say where things are • Talk about your family	• *Be*: simple present affirmative statements • Singular and plural nouns • Subject pronouns and possessive adjectives	• Ask about locations in a building • Numbers 1–10 • Give telephone numbers	• Stressed syllables • Pronunciation of *-s* and *-es* word endings	• Predict the topic: Read the title An article about lucky and unlucky numbers
2 **Carmen's Busy Day** page 19	• Say how you feel • Describe people • Pay the cashier • Say there's a mistake	• *Be*: simple present negative statements • *Be*: simple present *yes/no* questions	• Identify U.S. currency • Read prices • Read a receipt	• Pronunciation of negative contractions • Intonation in *yes/no* questions	• Understand the topic: What do you know? An online advice column about talking to your kids about money
3 **Oscar Is in Charge** page 33	• Say goodbye • Ask for help • Express likes and dislikes • Ask permission to leave work early	• *This, that, these, those* • Simple present: statements	• Read traffic signs • Read a supermarket flyer • Read and say the time	• Stressed words • Pronunciation of *th* sound	• Predict the topic: Look at pictures An article about E-bikes
4 **Wen Likes his Job** page 47	• Ask for something in a store • Follow two-step instructions • Talk about a favorite recipe • Talk about your schedule	• *Be*: Simple present questions with *Where* • Descriptive adjectives	• Identify parts of the body • Say the days of the week • Read a work schedule	• Pronunciation of words that begin with two consonants • Pronunciation of *do you*	• Predict the topic: Read headings An article about sleeping
5 **Saba Doesn't Feel Well** page 61	• Talk about the weather • Say how you feel • Make a medical appointment • Confirm personal information	• Simple present *yes/no* questions: *have, hurt* • *Be*: Simple present questions with *What*	• Identify months of the year • Say and write dates • Read an appointment card	• Intonation in questions and statements • Stress in months ending in *-er* and *-ary* • Pronunciation of groups of numbers	• Skimming An article about walk-in clinics

My English Lab

Vocabulary	Practical Skills	Writing	Unit Tests
Listening and Speaking	Grammar	Job-Seeking	Midterm Tests
Pronunciation	Reading		Final CASAS Test Prep

Writing Skills	Vocabulary ActiveTeach	Job-Seeking Skills	Career Pathways	CASAS Highlights	Common Core College and Career Readiness
• Capital and lowercase letters • Numbers	NA	NA	• Develop interpersonal relationships • Communicate clearly	0.1.2, 0.1.4, 0.1.5, 0.2.1, 0.2.2	NA
• Write an email to a friend	• Learning strategy: Group by meaning • Word list page 156	• Think about your job needs	• Develop interpersonal relationships • Manage others • Demonstrate resilience • Communicate clearly • Work as a team • Show concern • Ask for clarification	0.1.2, 0.1.4, 0.2.1, 0.2.3, 0.2.4, 2.1.8, 6.0.1, 4.1.6, 4.1.8, 4.4.4, 4.6.4, 4.8.1, 7.2.1, 7.2.2, 7.2.4	R.1, R.3 W.1, W.3 SL.K, SL.1, SL.3 L.1, L.2
• Give details	• Learning strategy: Use your first language • Word list page 156	• Assess your job skills	• Develop interpersonal relationships • Communicate clearly • Learn from mistakes • Help others • Show concern	0.1.2, 0.1.4, 0.1.8, 0.2.1, 0.2.3, 1.1.6, 1.2.1, 1.2.2, 1.3.8, 1.5.3, 1.8.1, 2.5.4, 4.1.6, 4.1.8, 4.6.5, 4.8.1, 4.8.3, 4.8.4, 7.2.1, 7.2.2	R.1, R.3, W.1, W.3 SL.K, SL.1, SL.3 L.1, L.2
• Write for a purpose	• Learning strategy: Group words by parts of speech • Word list page 157	• Look at job ads online	• Develop interpersonal relationships • Communicate clearly • Manage and help others • Ask for clarification • Offer solutions • Prioritize tasks	0.1.2, 0.1.4, 0.2.1, 0.2.3, 0.2.4, 1.2.1, 1.2.2, 1.3.8, 1.9.1, 1.9.2, 2.3.1, 4.1.3, 4.1.6, 4.4.1, 4.6.4, 4.8.1, 7.2.2, 7.2.4	R.1, R.2, R.3 W.1, W.3 SL.K, SL.1, SL.3 L.1, L.2
• Use correct tone	• Learning strategy: Recognize collocations • Word list page 157	• Look at job ads in the newspaper	• Develop interpersonal relationships • Communicate clearly • Manage and help others • Work as a team • Think on your feet • Offer solutions • Prioritize tasks	0.1.2, 0.1.7, 0.2.3, 2.3.2, 2.3.4, 3.1.1, 3.6.1, 3.6.3, 3.6.4, 4.1.3, 4.1.6, 4.1.8, 4.4.1, 4.4.3, 4.4.4, 4.6.4, 4.6.5, 4.8.1, 4.8.3, 4.8.4, 7.2.2, 7.2.4	R.1, R.2, R.3 W.1, W.3 SL.K, SL.1, SL.3 L.1, L.2
• Give instructions • Write instructions in the correct order	• Learning strategy: Write personal sentences • Word list page 158	• Complete a job application: Part 1	• Develop interpersonal relationships • Communicate clearly • Show concern • Give advice • Prioritize tasks	0.1.2, 0.1.8, 0.2.1, 0.2.3, 2.3.2, 2.5.3, 3.1.1, 3.1.2, 3.1.3, 3.5.9, 3.6.1, 3.6.3, 3.6.4, 4.1.2, 4.1.6, 4.8.1, 7.2.1, 7.2.2	R.1, R.2, R.3 W.1, W.3 SL.K, SL.1, SL.3 L.1, L.2

For complete correlations please visit www.pearsoneltusa.com/projectsuccess

Scope and Sequence 1

Unit	Listening/Speaking VIDEO	Grammar VIDEO	Practical Skills	Pronunciation	Reading Skills
6 **Saba Goes to the Doctor** page 75	• Change an appointment • Talk about your symptoms • Follow advice when you are sick • Call in sick	• Imperatives • *Should / shouldn't*	• Sign in at a medical office • Follow medical instructions • Read a medicine label and dosage	• Pronunciation of *a, an, for, of* • Pronunciation of *should / shouldn't*	• Scanning An article about kitchen cures
7 **Oscar Wants to Move** page 89	• Call about an apartment for rent • Talk about moving to a new apartment • Give directions • Talk about your apartment	• Possessive nouns • *There is/there are* statements	• Give an address • Read an apartment for rent ad • Read a map	• Pronunciation of vowels in stressed and unstressed syllables • Repeat words as a question to check understanding	• Paragraphs An article about couch surfing
8 **Wen's Surprise** page 103	• Call in late to work • Talk about your abilities • Talk about your weekend • Ask for and give prices	• *Can/can't* for ability • *Be, have, go*: simple past	• Identify places in the community • Read a bus schedule • Address an envelope	• Pronunciation of *can / can't* • Pronunciation of vowel sounds in *much* and *dollars*	• Point of view Restaurant reviews
9 **Truda Asks for Help** page 117	• Talk about good news and bad news • Report a housing problem • Talk about forms at work • Call 911 to report an emergency	• Present continuous: statements • Object pronouns	• Read a pay stub • Complete an emergency contact form • Read warning signs	• Show strong feeling • Link *is / are* with words before them	• Identify author's purpose An online article about what to do in an emergency
10 **Carmen Gets an Invitation** page 131	• Talk about clothing • Return something to the store • Order from a menu • Accept an invitation	• Simple present: *Wh-* questions • *Be going to*	• Read clothing sizes • Say why you are returning something • Read a menu	• Pronunciation of *and = 'n* • Pronunciation of *going to = gonna*	• Guess words from context An article about dining in the dark

My English Lab

Vocabulary
Listening and Speaking
Pronunciation

Practical Skills
Grammar
Reading

Writing
Job-Seeking

Unit Tests
Midterm Tests
Final CASAS Test Prep

Writing Skills	Vocabulary ActiveTeach	Job-Seeking Skills	Career Pathways	CASAS Highlights	Common Core College and Career Readiness
• Give advice • Use *should* to write advice	• Learning strategy: Groups words by number of syllables • Word list page 158	• Complete a job application: Part 2	• Communicate clearly • Think on your feet • Show concern • Give advice • Be self-aware • Offer solutions	0.1.2, 0.1.3, 0.1.7, 0.2.3, 2.5.3, 3.1.1, 3.1.2, 3.1.3, 3.5.9, 3.6.1, 3.6.3, 3.6.4, 4.1.2, 4.1.6, 4.8.1, 7.2.2	R.1, R.2, W.1, W.3 SL.K, SL.1, SL.3 L.1, L.2
• Give a main idea • The main idea is the most important idea in your writing.	• Learning strategy: Make word webs • Word list page 159	• Prepare for a job interview	• Develop interpersonal relationships • Communicate clearly • Ask for clarification • Offer solutions • Promote yourself in an interview	0.1.2, 0.2.1, 0.2.3, 1.4.1-2, 1.5.2, 2.2.5, 2.5.4, 4.1.6, 4.8.1, 7.2.1, 7.2.2	R.1, R.2, R.3 W.1, W.3 SL.K, SL.1, SL.3 L.1, L.2
• Write a narrative • A narrative is a story.	• Learning strategy: Draw pictures • Word list page 159	• Have a job interview: Part 1	• Manage others • Give praise • Work as a team • Ask for clarification • Offer solutions • Communicate a complaint • Promote yourself in an interview	0.1.2, 0.2.1, 0.2.3, 0.2.4, 2.2.2, 2.2.3, 2.6.1, 4.1.6, 4.4.1, 4.6.4, 4.8.1, 4.8.3, 7.2.1, 7.2.2	R.1, R.2 W.1, W.3 SL.K, SL.1, SL.3 L.1, L.2
• Express thanks • Give details in a thank you letter to say why you are writing	• Learning strategy: Group by context • Word list page 160	• Have a job interview: Part 2	• Manage others • Manage your emotions • Demonstrate resilience • Show concern • Communicate a complaint • Promote yourself in an interview	0.1.2, 0.2.2, 0.2.3, 1.4.1, 1.4.7, 2.1.2, 2.1.8, 4.1.6, 4.2.1, 4.3.1, 4.4.3, 4.6.5, 4.8.1, 4.8.4, 7.2.2, 7.2.4	R.1, R.2, R.3 W.1, W.3 SL.K, SL.1, SL.3 L.1, L.2
• Give an opinion • Use words such as *think* and *believe* to write about opinions and beliefs	• Learning strategy: Label objects • Word list page 160	• Get hired	• Develop interpersonal relationships • Communicate clearly • Help others • Offer solutions • Communicate a complaint	0.1.2, 0.1.4, 0.2.3, 1.1.4, 1.2.1, 1.3.3, 1.3.9, 1.8.1, 2.6.4, 4.1.6, 4.8.1, 4.8.3, 4.8.4, 7.2.2, 7.2.4	R.1, R.2, R.3 W.1, W.3 SL.K, SL.1, SL.3 L.1, L.2

Project Success is a dynamic six-level, four-skills multimedia course for adults and young adults. It offers a comprehensive and integrated program for false-beginner to low-advanced learners, with a classroom and online curriculum correlated to national and state standards.

KEY FEATURES

In developing this course we focused on our students' future aspirations, and on their current realities. Through inspiring stories of adults working and mastering life's challenges, we illustrate the skills and competencies adult English language learners need to participate fully and progress in their roles at home, work, school, and in the community. To create versatile and dynamic learning tools, we integrate digital features such as video, audio, and an online curriculum into one unified and comprehensive course. The result is *Project Success*: the first blended digital course designed for adult-education English language learners.

MULTIMEDIA: INSIDE AND OUTSIDE THE CLASSROOM

All *Project Success* materials are technologically integrated for seamless independent and classroom learning. The user-friendly digital interface will appeal to students who are already technologically adept, while providing full support for students who have less computer experience.

In class, the teacher uses the **ActiveTeach** DVD-ROM to project the lessons on the board. Video, audio, flashcards, conversation frameworks, checklists, comprehension questions, and other learning material are all available at the click of a button. Students use their print **Student Book** as they participate in class activities, take notes, and interact in group work.

Outside of class, students access their *Project Success* **eText** to review the videos, audio, and eFlashcards from class. They use their **MyEnglishLab** access code to get further practice online with new listenings and readings, additional practice activities, and video-based exercises.

A VARIETY OF WORKFORCE AND LIFE SKILLS

Each level of *Project Success* presents a different cast of characters at a different workplace. In each book, students learn instrumental language, employment, and educational skills as they watch the characters interact with co-workers, customers, family, and friends. As students move through the series, level by level, they learn about six important sectors in today's economy: food service, hospitality, healthcare, higher education, business, and retail.

The language and skills involved in daily life range from following directions, to phone conversations, to helping customers, to

asking permission to leave early. By representing a day in the life of a character, *Project Success* can introduce a diverse sampling of the content, language, and competencies involved in daily life and work. This approach allows students to learn diverse competencies and then practice them, in different settings and contexts, at different points in the curriculum.

VIDEO VIGNETTES

Each unit is organized around a series of short videos that follow one main character through his or her workday. In Listening and Speaking lessons, students watch the video together, see the character model a key competency in a realistic setting, and then practice the competency in pairs and groups. Discussion questions and group activities encourage students to identify and interpret the rich cultural content embedded in the video. The unit's grammar points are presented in the context of natural language in the video and then highlighted for more study and practice in a separate grammar lesson.

CRITICAL THINKING SKILLS

In the *What do you think?* activity at the end of nearly every lesson, students analyze, evaluate, infer, or relate content in the lesson to other contexts and situations.

A ROBUST ASSESSMENT STRAND

The series includes a rich assessment package that consists of unit review tests, midterms, and a CASAS-like final test. The tests assess students on CASAS objectives which are integrated into practical skills and listening strands.

The tests are available online or in a printable version on the ActiveTeach.

THE COMPONENTS:

ActiveTeach

This is a powerful digital platform for teachers. It blends a digital form of the Student Book with interactive whiteboard (IWB) software and printable support materials.

MyEnglishLab

This is a dynamic, easy-to-use online learning and assessment program that is integral to the *Project Success* curriculum. Original interactive activities extend student practice of vocabulary, listening, speaking, pronunciation, grammar, reading, writing, and practical skills from the classroom learning component.

eText

The eText is a digital version of the Student Book with all the audio and video integrated, and with a complete set of the pop-up eFlashcards.

WELCOME TO *PROJECT SUCCESS*!

Project Success is a six-level digital and print English program designed for you. It teaches English, employment, and learning skills for your success at work and school.

YOUR CLASSROOM LEARNING

Bring the Student Book to your classroom to learn new material and to practice with your classmates in groups. Every unit has:

- Four video-based lessons for your listening and speaking skills
- Two practical skills lessons
- Two grammar lessons
- One lesson for getting a job
- One lesson for writing
- One lesson for reading
- One review page

YOUR ONLINE LEARNING

Your access code is on the front cover of your Student Book. Use the access code to go online. There you will find eText and MyEnglishLab.

Go to your eText to review what you learned in class. You can watch the videos again, listen to audio, and review the Vocabulary Flashcards.

Go to MyEnglishLab online to practice what you learned in class. MyEnglishLab has:

- Extra listening practice
- Extra reading practice
- Extra grammar practice
- Extra writing practice
- Extra practice of vocabulary skills
- Extra practice of life skills
- Additional video-based exercises
- "Record and compare," so you can record yourself and listen to your own pronunciation
- Instant feedback
- Job-seeking activities

Welcome Unit

MEET YOUR CLASSMATES

A ◀))) **Listen. Listen and repeat.**

A: Hello. I'm Peter.

B: Hi. I'm Rosa.

A: Nice to meet you.

B: Nice to meet you, too.

A: Where are you from, Rosa?

B: I'm from Mexico. Where are you from?

A: I'm from Poland.

B Walk around the room. Meet your classmates.

C ◀))) **Look at the student identification (ID) card. Listen and repeat.**

Falls Adult School

Name:	Marina Petrova
Teacher's name:	Betsy Florez
Class: ESL 1	Room: 212

Student Identification Card

D Complete the form for your student ID card.

New Student Identification Card

School name: _____

Your name: _____ Class: _____

Teacher's name: _____ Room: _____

E **PAIRS** Show your form to your partner.

LEARN CLASSROOM LANGUAGE

A ◀))) Listen and repeat.

1. Take out your book.

2. Point to the picture.

3. Read the exercise.

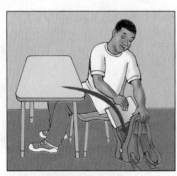
4. Put away your book.

5. Look at the board.

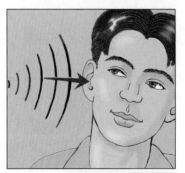
6. Listen.

7. Open your notebook.

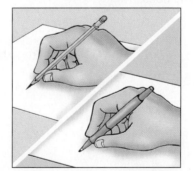
8. Use a pencil. / Use a pen.

9. Write your name.

B ◀))) Listen. Follow the instructions.

C ◀))) Listen and repeat.

Can you repeat that, please?

I'm sorry. I don't understand.

What page?

How do you say ____ in English?

LEARN ABOUT *PROJECT SUCCESS*

A **Learn about your book.**

1. Look at the cover of your book. What is the title of your book?
2. Look at the inside front cover. Where is the access code?
3. See page iii. How many units are in your book?
4. See page 162. Where is your country on the map?

B **Meet the characters in your book.**
They all work at Fresh Foods supermarket.

I'm Oscar Perez.
I'm the produce manager.

I'm Wen Li. I'm an associate
in the produce department.
Oscar is my boss.

I'm Truda Mazur.
I'm a new deli worker.

I'm Saba Andarge. I'm a
customer service representative.

I'm Carmen Vasquez.
I'm a cashier.

1 Truda's New Job

MY GOALS

- ☐ Introduce myself
- ☐ Say what I do
- ☐ Say where things are
- ☐ Ask about locations in a building
- ☐ Talk about my family
- ☐ Give my phone number
- ☐ Think about my job needs

Go to MyEnglishLab for more practice after each lesson.

Truda Mazur

Truda *Today*
I start my new job today.
I'm really excited!

LISTENING AND SPEAKING

1 Introduce yourself

GET READY

Oscar and Truda are at the supermarket.
Guess. What are they doing?

WATCH

A ▪◀ **Watch the video.**
Was your guess correct?

B ▪◀ **Watch the video again. Circle the answer.**

1. Oscar and Truda are _____.
  a. friends   **b.** coworkers

2. Truda is a new _____.
  a. customer   **b.** employee

C **Complete the sentences about the video. Use the words from the box.**

> first   help   introduce

1. Oscar wants to _____ Truda.

2. It is Truda's _____ day of work.

3. Truda and Oscar _____ themselves.

CONVERSATION

A ▪◀ **Watch part of the video. Complete the conversation.**

Oscar: _____. I'm Oscar Perez.

Truda: _____. I'm Truda Mazur.

Oscar: Nice to meet you.

Truda: I'm sorry. What's your name again, please?

Oscar: Oscar.

Truda: Nice to meet you, Oscar.

B ◀))) **Listen and repeat.**

C **PAIRS Practice the conversation. Use your own names.**

WHAT DO YOU THINK?

What do people say and do in the U.S. when they meet each other for
the first time at work? Is it the same or different in your country?

LISTENING AND SPEAKING

2 Say what you do

GET READY

Oscar and Truda work at the Fresh Foods supermarket.

Guess. What do you think they do?

WATCH

A ■◀ **Watch the video.**
Was your guess correct?

B ■◀ **Watch the video again.**
Read the sentences. Circle the correct answers.

1. Truda's job is in the _____.
   a. bakery   **b.** produce department   **c.** deli

2. Oscar's job is in the _____.
   a. bakery   **b.** produce department   **c.** deli

3. Joe is a _____.
   a. produce associate   **b.** produce manager   **c.** deli worker

CONVERSATION

A ■◀ **Watch part of the video. Complete the conversation.**

Oscar: Which department do you work in, Truda?

Truda: In the _____.
               ★

Oscar: Oh! You're the new _____.
                     ★★
Welcome to Fresh Foods!

Truda: Thank you. What do you do, Oscar?

Oscar: I'm the produce manager.

> **Pronunciation Note**
>
> A syllable is a part of a word: wel·come. One syllable in a word is stressed: **wel**·come. The stressed syllable is long and loud.
>
> ◀ッ) **Listen and repeat.**
>
> **wel**·come   **del**·i   a·**gain**
>
> **man**·a·ger   de·**part**·ment   in·tro·**duce**

B ◀ッ) **Listen and repeat.**

C **PAIRS** Practice the conversation. Use your own names.

D **PAIRS** Practice the conversation again.
Use different departments and jobs.

WHAT DO YOU THINK?

GROUPS It's Truda's first day at work. How do you think she feels?

Be: Simple present affirmative statements

STUDY *Be:* Simple present affirmative statements

Full Form		
I	**am**	
He She	**is**	a manager.
You	**are**	
Oscar and I We		
	are	managers.
Oscar and Jim They		

Contractions	
I'**m** He'**s** She'**s** You'**re**	a manager.
You'**re** We'**re** They'**re**	managers.

> **Grammar Note**
>
> Use *it is* or *it's* to talk about something (not someone).
> *Where's the supermarket?*
> ***It is** on Bank Street.*
> ***It's** on Bank Street.*

PRACTICE

A **Rewrite the sentences. Change the underlined words. Use the words from the box.**

> I'm   He's   She's   ~~It's~~   We're   They're

1. <u>Today</u> is my first day.   It's my first day.

2. <u>Oscar and Jim</u> are managers.   _____

3. <u>Truda</u> is a deli worker.   _____

4. <u>I</u> am a dairy associate.   _____

5. <u>Joe</u> is a dairy associate.   _____

6. <u>We</u> are coworkers at Fresh Foods. _____

B **Complete the sentences. Use the correct form of *be*. Use contractions.**

1. Joe _____*is*_____ a produce clerk. _____*He's*_____ a good worker.

2. Sam and Pete _____ bakers. _____ friends.

3. She _____ a cashier. _____ a new employee.

4. We _____ customers. _____ happy to shop here.

5. You _____ a deli worker. _____ a new worker.

6. I _____ a boss. _____ a deli manager.

WHAT ABOUT YOU?

PAIRS Ask your partner *What do you do?*
Use real or made-up information to answer.

> What do you do?
>
> I'm a cashier.

LISTENING AND SPEAKING

4

Say where things are

GET READY

Jim is Truda's manager.

Guess. What are they talking about?

WATCH

A ■◀ **Watch the video. Was your guess correct?**

B ■◀ **Watch the video again. Read the sentences. Circle *True* or *False*. Then correct the false sentences.**

1.	Jim and Truda are in the produce department.	True	False
2.	The spoons and knives are in different drawers.	True	False
3.	There are three scales.	True	False
4.	The gloves are above the scales.	True	False
5.	Truda's morning break is 15 minutes.	True	False

CONVERSATION

A ■◀ **Watch part of the video. Complete the conversation.**

Jim: What else can I show you?

Truda: I see the plastic bags.

Where are the _____?
★

Jim: They're _____ the counter.
★★

Truda: OK. And where are boxes for take-out orders?

Jim: They're over here.

Truda: Do you have more if we run out?

Jim: Yes, I keep more in the back.

B ◀)) **Listen and repeat.**

C **PAIRS Practice the conversation.**

D **PAIRS Practice the conversation again.**
Use different supplies and different places.

Pronunciation Note

Add an extra syllable for the *-es* ending after sounds like /s/, /ʃ/, and /tʃ/:
slic·**es**, dish·**es**, sandwich·**es**.
Do not add an extra syllable for *-s* or *-es* after most other sounds.

◀)) **Listen and repeat.**

bags	scales	knives
gloves	minutes	boxes

WHAT DO YOU THINK?

Truda is a new employee. She needs to ask Jim many questions.
What should Truda do if she doesn't understand something?

Singular and plural nouns

STUDY Singular and plural nouns

Singular Nouns	Plural Nouns
Oscar is a **manager**.	Oscar and Jim are **managers**.
The **customer** is in the supermarket.	The **customers** are in the supermarket.
The **bag** is on the counter.	The **bags** are on the counter.

Grammar Note

Add **-s** to form most plural nouns.

Add **-es** to words that end in s, sh, ch, and x: box ⟶ boxes

If a word ends in **-fe**, change the f to v and add **-es**: knife ⟶ knives

Some plural nouns are irregular:

man ⟶ men   woman ⟶ women   child ⟶ children

PRACTICE

A   **Underline the correct words.**

1. Truda is a new <u>deli worker</u> / deli workers.

2. Joe is an associate / associates.

3. Truda and Joe are coworker / coworkers.

4. Jim is the deli manager / deli managers.

5. Here are some plastic glove / gloves.

6. Truda is on a break / breaks now.

B   **Jim is making a list for the deli department. Write the correct form of the nouns.**

5 small _forks_   4 deli _____
         fork   apron

2 large _____   1 serving _____
            knife   spoon

1 new _____   3 _____ of gloves
          scale   box

WHAT ABOUT YOU?

PAIRS Look around. What is in your classroom, in your backpack, or on your desk? Make a list of 8 things. Use singular and plural nouns.

PRACTICAL SKILLS

6 Ask about locations in a building

GET READY

You are in the supermarket. You want to find the bakery. What do you do?

LOCATIONS IN A BUILDING

A ◀))) **Listen and point. Listen and repeat.**

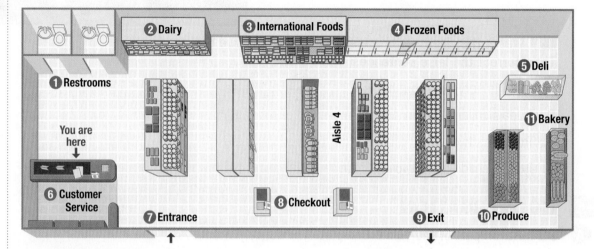

B **Read the conversation. What location on the map does the speaker ask about? Complete the conversation.**

A: Excuse me. Which way is the _____ section?

B: It's at the back of the store.
Walk to Aisle 4 and then go left.
It's next to the international foods.

A: Next to the international foods?

B: Yes.

A: Thank you.

> **Speaking Note**
>
> Repeat information to make sure you understand correctly.
> *Next to the international foods?*

C ◀))) **Listen and check your answer. Then practice the conversation with a classmate.**

ROLE PLAY

PAIRS Look at the map. Ask for locations and give directions. Take turns.
Use the words in the boxes.

Locations	Directions
the deli	at the front of the store
the international section	at the back of the store
the dairy section	go to the right / go to the left
the restrooms	next to
	on the right / on the left

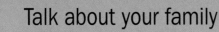

LISTENING AND SPEAKING

7

Talk about your family

GET READY

Saba and Truda are taking a break.

Do you talk about your family with your coworkers?

WATCH

◼◀ **Watch the video. Read the sentences. Circle *True* or *False*. Then correct the false sentences.**

1.	Truda is nervous about her job.	True	False
2.	Truda's children are in school.	True	False
3.	Truda has two sons.	True	False
4.	Truda's children are two and four.	True	False

CONVERSATION

A ◼◀ **Watch part of the video. Complete the conversation.**

Saba: What's wrong?

Truda: It's my family. My children are at home without me, so I feel bad.

Saba: Your children are little? How old are they?

Truda: My daughter is two and my son is four.

Saba: Oh, cute! But they aren't home alone. I'm sure you have a good babysitter.

Truda: Yes, my sister. But it's their first day without me.

Saba: They'll be fine!

Truda: I called them and everything is _____.
★

Saba: _____
★★

B ◀)) **Listen and repeat.**

C **PAIRS** Practice the conversation.

D **PAIRS** Practice the conversation again. Use different words and expressions.

WHAT DO YOU THINK?

GROUPS Truda and Saba are talking about their families.
What topics are OK for the workplace?
What topics are not OK?

> It's not OK to ask about salaries . . .

GRAMMAR

8 Subject pronouns and possessive adjectives

STUDY Subject pronouns and possessive adjectives

Subject Pronouns		
I	am	
You	are	
He	is	married.
She		
We	are	
They		

Possessive Adjectives		
My		
Your		
His	children	are at home.
Her		
Our		
Their		

Grammar Note

Use *it* for things.
The possessive adjective is *its*.

The store has a new name.
Its new name is Caramel Cakes.

PRACTICE

A **Underline the correct words.**

1. Do you like my / <u>your</u> new job?

2. Truda has two children. His / Her children are with the babysitter.

3. I'm a baker. My / Your job is at a supermarket.

4. Carmen and I are cashiers. Our / Their schedules are the same.

5. Truda works in the deli. Jim is her / his manager.

B **Complete the message. Use the words from the box. Use one word two times.**

my   your   his   her   ~~We~~   She   He

Hi, Liam. Do you remember me? This is Hana Fox. _____We_____ met last month at a party.
1.

I'm calling about _____ good friend Sara. _____ is looking for a nice guy. She
2.   3.

broke up with _____ boyfriend last month. So I called Joe Tretin. _____ gave me
4.   5.

_____ number. So about my friend . . . She's a lot of fun. _____ favorite thing is
6.   7.

movies. She likes kids. She's looking for a guy who wants _____ own family someday.
8.

So . . . do you want to meet her? Give me a call.

C ◀)) **Listen and check your answers.**

WHAT ABOUT YOU?

PAIRS Tell your partner about yourself and your family.

How old are your children?

_____ children are
_____ years old.

What's your name?

Where are you from?

_____ name is _____.

_____ from _____.

GET READY

You need someone's telephone number. Where can you find it?

TELEPHONE NUMBERS

A ◀))) **Listen and read.**
Then listen and repeat the telephone numbers.

1.

Fresh Foods

703-555-8660

Thank you for shopping with us!

2.

Fresh Foods
Job Application

Name: _Su Park_

Phone number: _703-555-9336_

B ◀))) **Listen. Complete the phone numbers.**

1. **A:** What's your home phone number?

   B: __ __ __ – 555 – __ __ __ __.

2. **A:** My cell number is __ __ __ – 555 – __ __ __ __.

   B: Can you repeat that, please?

   A: Yes. It's __ __ __ – 555 – __ __ __ __.

3. **A:** My work number is __ __ __ – 555 – __ __ __ __.

   B: So, that's __ __ __ – 555 – __ __ __ __.

   A: Yes, that's correct.

> **Speaking Note**
>
> Ask for repetition.
> Say: *Can you repeat that, please?*

C ◀))) **Listen again and check your answers.**

D **Fill out the form with your own information.**

Fresh Foods
Job Application

Name: _____

Phone number: _____

ROLE PLAY

PAIRS Make new conversations. Take turns asking for phone numbers.
Use real or made-up information.

10 Write an email to a friend

STUDY THE MODEL

A **Read the email. Who is writing the email? Who is she writing to?**

○ ○ ○

From: Truda Mazur
Date: March 18, 2014 7:30 P.M.

Hi, Donna:

I have good news! I have a new job. I'm a deli worker at a supermarket. It's called Fresh Foods. Jim is my boss. He's helpful. The deli is always busy. My coworkers are nice. I usually have lunch with Saba. She's a customer service representative. I really like my new job!

I have to go now. Email me soon!

Truda

B **Read the Writing Tip. Read Truda's email again. What is the topic?**

a. Truda's new coworkers

b. Truda's new job

c. Truda's new boss

> **Writing Tip**
>
> The **topic** of an email is what you are writing about.

BEFORE YOU WRITE

PAIRS Think about a job you have or imagine a new job. Answer these questions.

1. What is the job?

_____

2. Where is the job?

_____

3. Who do you work for?

_____

4. Who do you work with?

_____

WRITE

Write to a friend about the job. Use your information.
Study Truda's email and the Writing Tip.

11 Predict the topic: Read the title

GET READY

Look at the title. This article is probably about _____.

a. baseball players **b.** weddings **c.** lucky numbers

> **Reading Skill**
>
> Read the title first. It can help you predict—guess—what you will read about.

READD

◀))) **Listen and read the article. What are the four numbers in this article?**

What's Your Number?

Ana Long thinks the number 7 is lucky. She has seven brothers and sisters. Her apartment number is 7. Ana wants to get married on July 7. She thinks it will bring good luck.

People around the world believe numbers can be lucky or unlucky. Sometimes the sound of the number makes it lucky or unlucky. For example, in China the number 8 is a lucky number. In Chinese it sounds like the word 八. This word means to have a lot of money. In Japan, the number 4 is unlucky. It has the sound *shi*. In Japanese the word 死 means death. Baseball players don't have the number 4 on their uniforms.

In the United States, people think the number 13 is very unlucky. Many buildings do not have a 13th floor. People also think that any Friday the 13th is a very unlucky day.

Are numbers lucky or unlucky? What do you think?

AFTER YOU READ

Read the article again. Complete the chart.

Country	Number	Lucky	Unlucky
China		✓	
	4		
United States			✓

WHAT DO YOU THINK?

GROUPS Talk about your country. Do people believe numbers are lucky or unlucky? Which numbers?

JOB-SEEKING SKILLS
Think about your job needs

Sara *Today*
I'm Sara Moreno, Truda's friend. She told me there are jobs at Fresh Foods.

GET READY

Sarah is looking for a job.
What are some things to think about when you are looking for a job?

JOB NEEDS

A 🔊 **Listen. Sara is talking about her job needs. Look at the form for job seekers. Check [✓] the information that matches Sara's needs.**

I need a job that is . . .
- [ ] part-time
- [ ] in the daytime
- [ ] close to home
- [ ] indoors
- [ ] the same every day
- [ ] full-time
- [ ] at night
- [ ] near transportation
- [ ] outdoors
- [ ] is flexible

B **Think about your job needs. Write your information. Then tell a partner.**

1. I need a _____ job.
   full-time / part-time

2. I need to work _____.
   in the daytime / at night

3. I can work _____.
   close to home / near transportation

4. I want to work _____.
   indoors / outdoors

5. I need a job that is _____.
   the same every day / flexible

C **PAIRS Talk about your job needs. Take turns.**

A: What kind of job do you need?

B: I need a _____.

PUT YOUR IDEAS TO WORK

GROUPS Think about your list of job needs in Exercise B.
Which need is the most important for you?
Then share your ideas with the group.

GRAMMAR

In this unit, you studied:

- *Be:* Simple present affirmative statements
- Singular and plural nouns
- Subject pronouns and possessive adjectives

See page 145 for your Grammar Review.

VOCABULARY See page 156 for the Unit 1 Vocabulary.

Vocabulary Learning Strategy: Group by meaning

A Choose words from the list and put them into these groups:

Words for jobs	Words for things	Words for women	Words for men
baker	bag	wife	father

B Underline 5 words from Exercise A. Write a sentence with each word.

SPELLING See page 156 for the Unit 1 Vocabulary.

CLASS Choose 10 words for a spelling test.

LISTENING PLUS

A Watch each video.
Write the story of Truda's day on a separate piece of paper.

It's Truda's first day at Fresh Foods supermarket. She is the new deli worker.

B PAIRS Review the conversation in Lesson 2 (see page 7).
Role play the conversation for the class.

NOW I CAN

PAIRS See page 5 for the Unit 1 Goals. Check ☑ the things you can do.
Underline the things you want to study more. Tell your partner.

I can _____. I need more practice with _____.

2 Carmen's Busy Day

MY GOALS

- ☐ Say how I feel
- ☐ Describe people
- ☐ Identify U.S. currency
- ☐ Read prices
- ☐ Pay the cashier
- ☐ Say there's a mistake
- ☐ Read a receipt
- ☐ Assess my job skills

Go to MyEnglishLab for more practice after each lesson.

Carmen Vasquez

Carmen   *Today*

I don't like to make mistakes, but sometimes it happens. I always say I'm sorry!

1 Say how you feel

Carmen and Saba arrive at work.

Guess. What are they talking about?

WATCH

A ■◀ Watch the video. Was your guess correct?

B ■◀ Watch the video again. Read the sentences. Circle *True* or *False*.
Then correct the false sentences.

1.	Carmen is sick.	True	False
2.	Oscar is happy.	True	False
3.	One worker in Oscar's department is out sick.	True	False
4.	Saba and Carmen make plans to have lunch.	True	False

C Check [✓] the things Carmen and Saba talk about.

☐ Oscar's problem ☐ late employees

☐ Oscar's health ☐ sick employees

CONVERSATION

A ■◀ Watch part of the video. Complete the conversation.

Carmen: Good morning, Saba.

Saba: Hi, Carmen. How are you?

Carmen: I'm _____.
　　　　　　　　　　　★

Saba: That's good. But poor Oscar!

Carmen: What's wrong?

Saba: He's _____. Two workers
　　　　　　　　　　★★
in his department aren't here today.

> **Pronunciation Note**
>
> Notice the pronunciation of the negative contractions. The /t/ sound at the end is often quiet.
>
> ◀))) **Listen and repeat.**
> They aren't here today.
> I don't know.
> It isn't easy.

B ◀))) **Listen and repeat.**

C PAIRS Practice the conversation. Use your own names.

D PAIRS Practice the conversation again. Use different ways to answer
How are you? and express feelings.

WHAT DO YOU THINK?

GROUPS Two workers in Oscar's department are out sick today. What can he do?

Be: Simple present negative statements

STUDY *Be:* Simple present negative statements

Full Form

I	**am not**	busy.
You	**are not**	
He		
She	**is not**	married.
Joe		
You		
They	**are not**	cashiers.
We		
The store	**is not**	open today.
It		

Contractions

I'**m not**	busy.
You'**re not**	
He'**s not**	
She'**s not**	married.
Joe'**s not**	
You'**re not**	
They'**re not**	cashiers.
We'**re not**	
It'**s not**	open today.

Grammar Note

More negative
contractions
You **aren't**
He **isn't**
She **isn't**
The store **isn't**
It **isn't**
You **aren't**
They **aren't**
We **aren't**

PRACTICE

A **Read each sentence. Then write two negative sentences. Write on a piece of paper.**

1. You're a cashier.

You are not a cashier.
You're not a cashier.

2. Jim and Truda are sick.

3. You and I are managers.

4. The scale is on the shelf.

5. Carmen is upset.

B **Saba's husband, Kaleb, is telling her about his day at work. Underline the correct words.**

Well, **today we're not / today isn't** a good day. Mike is bored. **He's not / They're not** busy.
   1.   2.

Sue and Maria are upset. **We're not / They're not** happy with their boss. Fatima and I
                                                        3.

are tired, and **we're not / you're not** feeling well. John feels bad, too. **It's not / He's not**
                              4.   5.

here today, so I have a lot of work. **I'm / You're** stressed!
                                                          6.

WHAT ABOUT YOU?

GROUPS Make sentences about you and your classmates.
Choose words from the box. Use the negative form of *be.*

(busy   happy   hungry   sick   stressed   tired   upset)

(I'm not busy.)   (Abdul is not upset.)

LISTENING AND SPEAKING

3 Describe people

GET READY

Carmen and Saba are talking about a new coworker. What do you talk about with your coworkers or your classmates?

WATCH

■◀ Watch the video. Read the sentences. Circle the correct answers.

1. Carmen and Saba are _____.
   a. taking a break   b. working   c. helping a customer

2. Carmen is _____.
   a. upset   b. busy   c. hungry

3. Carmen did not meet the new _____.
   a. manager   b. coworker   c. customer

CONVERSATION

A **■◀ Watch part of the video. Complete the conversation.**

Saba: So, did you meet Truda, the new deli worker?

Carmen: I don't think so. What does she look like?

Saba: She's _____ and has blond hair.
                            ★

Carmen: Is she in the deli today?

Saba: Yes, she is.

Carmen: I didn't meet her. I'll say hi to her _____.
                                              ★★

B ◀)) Listen and repeat.

C PAIRS Practice the conversation.

D PAIRS Practice the conversation again. Use different descriptions and time words.

WHAT DO YOU THINK?

GROUPS Carmen meets her new coworker, Truda, after lunch.
The next day Carmen cannot remember Truda's name. What can she do?

> She can say, "I'm sorry. Please tell me your name again."

4

Be: Simple present yes / no questions

○○○○○○

STUDY Be: Simple present yes / no questions

Questions		
Are	you	
Is	Joe	
	he	
	she	tall?
Are	you	
	they	
	we	

Short Answers					
	I	am.			I'm not.
	he				he's not.
		is.			
Yes,	she		No,		she's not.
	we				we're not.
	they	are.			they're not.
	you				you're not.

Grammar Note

More negative short answers

you aren't.
he isn't.
No, she isn't.
we aren't.
they aren't.

○○○○○○

PRACTICE

A Complete the questions. Use *is* and *are*.

1. **A:** _____Is_____ he a produce associate?
   B: No, he's not.

2. **A:** _____ they new employees?
   B: Yes, they are.

3. **A:** _____ the knife in the drawer?
   B: Yes, it is.

4. **A:** _____ we late for work?
   B: No, we aren't.

5. **A:** _____ she in her 20s?
   B: No, she isn't.

B ◀)) Listen and check your answers. Then practice the conversations with a classmate.

C Carmen is talking to Truda. Complete the conversation.

Carmen: _____Are_____ you the new deli worker?
 1.

Truda: Yes, _____I am_____.
 2.

Carmen: _____ Jim your manager?
 3.

Truda: Yes, _____. I like him a lot.
 4.

Carmen: That's good. _____ you and Jim busy today?
 5.

Truda: No, _____.
 6.

WHAT ABOUT YOU?

PAIRS Take turns. Ask and answer *yes / no* questions about a person in your family. Use short answers.

Is he young?

No, he's not.

Is he tall?

Yes, he is.

PRACTICAL SKILLS

Identify U.S. currency

GET READY

How do you pay at a store? With cash? With a credit card? By check? Give examples.

U.S. CURRENCY

A ◀))) **Listen and point. Listen and repeat.**

one dollar ($1.00)

five dollars ($5.00)

ten dollars ($10.00)

twenty dollars ($20.00)

B ◀))) **Listen and point. Listen and repeat.**

a penny (1¢)   a nickel (5¢)   a dime (10¢)   a quarter (25¢)

Speaking Note

If you don't hear an amount, say:

Can you say that again?

Can you write that for me?

C **Count the coins and bills. How much money is it? Write the totals.**

1. _____   2. _____

3. _____   4. _____

WHAT DO YOU THINK?

GROUPS When you are shopping, do you check the price before you buy something? Give examples of products you buy and how much you pay.

○○○○○○ **GET READY** What kinds of fruits and vegetables do you buy at the store?

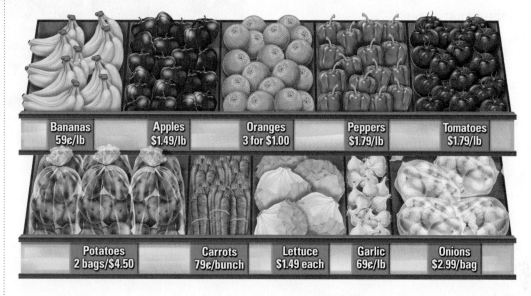

| Bananas 59¢/lb | Apples $1.49/lb | Oranges 3 for $1.00 | Peppers $1.79/lb | Tomatoes $1.79/lb |
| Potatoes 2 bags/$4.50 | Carrots 79¢/bunch | Lettuce $1.49 each | Garlic 69¢/lb | Onions $2.99/bag |

○○○○○○ **PRICES**

A **Look at the picture. Circle *True* or *False*. Correct the false statements.**

1. Tomatoes are $1.79 each.   True   False

2. Lettuce is $1.49 a pound.   True   False

3. Oranges are 3 for $1.   True   False

4. Garlic is 69¢ each.   True   False

5. Potatoes are 2 bags for $4.50.   True   False

B ◀))) **Listen. Circle the prices you hear.**

1. 59¢   89¢   79¢   **4.** $1.29 $2.79 $2.99

2. $2.49 $1.49 $4.99   **5.** $1.09 $1.79 $2.79

3. 90¢   70¢   79¢

C **PAIRS Look at the picture. Make new conversations.**

A: How much is the _____?

B: _____

A: How much are the _____?

B: _____

> **Speaking Note**
>
> Say: *Two ninety* or
> *Two dollars and ninety cents.*
>
> Say: *Four fifty* or
> *Four dollars and fifty cents.*

WHAT DO YOU THINK?

PAIRS Think about the prices of fruits and vegetables in your country.
Are they the same as or different from prices in the U.S.?

7 Pay the cashier

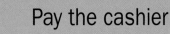

 GET READY

Look at the picture. Guess.

What is the customer asking Carmen?

WATCH

A ◼◀ **Watch the video. Was your guess correct?**

B ◼◀ **Watch the video again. Complete the sentences. Use the words from the box.**

> card   check   credit   on sale

1. Do you have a Fresh Foods _____?

2. Can you please do a price _____?

3. I think these are _____.

4. Is that _____ or debit?

CONVERSATION

A ◼◀ **Watch part of the video. Complete the conversation.**

Carmen: Hello. Do you have a Fresh Foods card?

Customer: Yes, I do. Here you go.

Carmen: Any coupons?

Customer: No. Can you please do a price check?

I think these are _____.
★

Carmen: Yes, you're right.

Customer: OK. I'll take them.

Carmen: OK, your total is $_____.
★★

Pronunciation Note

In *yes / no* questions, the voice usually goes up at the end.

◀ঙ) **Listen and repeat.**

Do you have a Fresh **Foods** card?

Can you please do a **price** check?

Any **cou**pons?

B ◀ঙ) **Listen and repeat.**

C PAIRS **Practice the conversation.**

D PAIRS **Practice the conversation again. Use different prices.**

WHAT DO YOU THINK?

PAIRS You are at the supermarket. You don't have your grocery card.
What do you do? Discuss.

> Go to the customer service desk.

> Pay the full price.

> Tell the cashier.

LISTENING AND SPEAKING

Say there's a mistake

GET READY

Carmen makes a mistake.

Guess. What is the mistake?

WATCH

A ◼◀ **Watch the video. Was your guess correct?**

B ◼◀ **Watch the video again. Put the sentences in order. Write 1, 2, 3, and 4.**

_____ The customer says, "There's a mistake."

_____ Carmen gives the customer the correct change.

_____ Carmen says, "I'm sorry!"

_____ Carmen gives the customer the wrong change.

C **Read the question about the video. Circle the answer.**

Carmen says, "Have a good day."
The customer says, "You do the same."
She means, "_____."

a. You, too   **b.** I will

CONVERSATION

A ◼◀ **Watch part of the video. Complete the conversation.**

Carmen: Your total is $5.67.

Customer: Here's a twenty.

Carmen: Here's your receipt. And your change is $14.33.

Customer: Excuse me. There's _____.
                This change is not correct. ★

Carmen: Oh. _____!
                         ★★

B ◀)) **Listen and repeat.**

C **PAIRS** **Practice the conversation.**

D **PAIRS** **Practice the conversation again. Use different words to show and apologize for mistakes.**

WHAT DO YOU THINK?

PAIRS Carmen apologizes and gives the customer the correct change.
Talk about different jobs and the mistakes a worker can make.
Give examples of mistakes. Say how the worker can apologize.

9 Read a receipt

GET READY

Think about the stores you shop at.
Do they give receipts?

RECEIPTS

A Read the receipt. Answer the questions.

1. What is the date?

_____

2. What is the store phone number?

_____

3. How much are the potatoes the customer bought?

_____

4. How much is one bag of carrots?

_____

5. How much tax did the customer pay?

_____

6. Did the customer pay with cash or credit card?

_____

7. How much change did the customer get back?

_____

Fresh Foods

Supermarket
Alexandria, VA
703-555-8660
06-17-2014 5:36 P.M.

Potatoes	
1 bag @ 2 for $5.00	$ 2.50
Bananas	
1 lb @ $.43/lb.	$ .43
Pineapple	
1 @ $2.99	$ 2.99
Carrots	
2 bags @ $1.19/bag	$ 2.38
Peppers	
6 @ 3 for $1.25	$ 2.50
Subtotal	$10.80
Tax 5% on	10.80
	$ .54
TOTAL	**$11.34**
CASH PAID	**$20.00**
CHANGE DUE	**$ 8.66**

B Read the receipt again. Write the information.

Tom stops at ____Fresh Foods____ supermarket on his way home from work. He
                        1.

buys a bag of _____ for $2.50. He buys _____ peppers for
                    2.   3.

$2.50. He buys a pineapple for $_____. His total is $_____.
                                   4.   5.

He pays with _____. His change is $_____.
                  6.   7.

C 🔊 **Listen and check your answers.**

WHAT DO YOU THINK?

GROUPS Do you save your receipts? Why or why not?

> I save my receipts. I check them later.

STUDY THE MODEL

A   **Read Carmen's email to her friend Jennifer.
What does Carmen ask Jennifer to do?**

Hi, Jennifer,

I'm so happy you can pick up my brother Dan at the airport
next week. You're a good friend.

Do you remember Dan? He's <u>tall</u> and good-looking. He has
brown hair and blue eyes. He usually wears jeans. He also
wears a long green overcoat. He often carries a red backpack.

Call me if you don't see him.

Thanks!

Carmen

B   **Read the Writing Tip. Read the email again.
Look for the details about Dan. Underline them.**

> **Writing Tip**
>
> **Details** give information
> about your topic.
> Details can describe a
> person, place, or thing.

BEFORE YOU WRITE

PAIRS Imagine. A family member is coming to visit you.
Say who the person is. Complete the word web. Use real or
made-up information. Give details to describe the person.

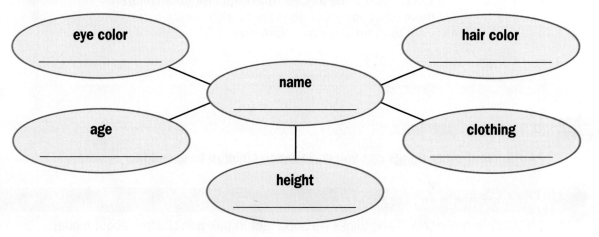

WRITE

Write to a friend on a separate piece of paper. Ask him or
her to pick up your family member. Use the details from
your word web. Study Carmen's email and the Writing Tip.

Understand the topic: What do you know?

GET READY

How do you save money? Give examples.

READ

◀))) **Listen and read the question and answer on the web page. Who are Robert and Silvia?**

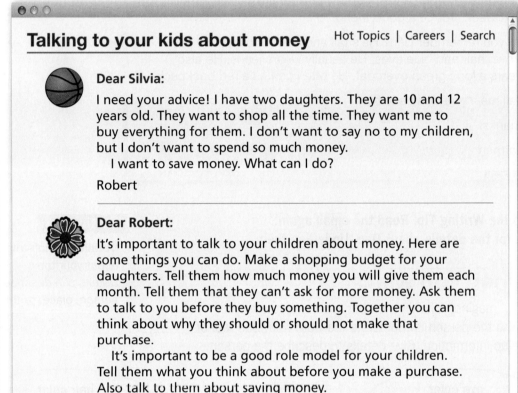

Talking to your kids about money   Hot Topics | Careers | Search

Dear Silvia:

I need your advice! I have two daughters. They are 10 and 12 years old. They want to shop all the time. They want me to buy everything for them. I don't want to say no to my children, but I don't want to spend so much money.
     I want to save money. What can I do?

Robert

Dear Robert:

It's important to talk to your children about money. Here are some things you can do. Make a shopping budget for your daughters. Tell them how much money you will give them each month. Tell them that they can't ask for more money. Ask them to talk to you before they buy something. Together you can think about why they should or should not make that purchase.
     It's important to be a good role model for your children. Tell them what you think about before you make a purchase. Also talk to them about saving money.

Silvia

AFTER YOU READ

PAIRS What other things can you do to teach children to spend money wisely?

WHAT DO YOU THINK?

GROUPS In the article, Silvia thinks it's important to talk with children about money. Why is it important to start this conversation early? Give examples.

JOB-SEEKING SKILLS

Assess your job skills

Sara   *Today*
I want to apply for a job.
I have work experience
as a cashier and a deli
worker.

GET READY

Sara worked as a deli worker and a cashier. What job skills do you think she has?

JOB SKILLS

A 🔊)) **Listen. Sara is talking about her job skills and personal traits.
Check [✓] the information you hear.**

Skills	Personal Traits
☐ use a computer	☐ work alone
☐ wrap meat	☐ work with people
☐ use a cash register	☐ work with machines
☐ stock shelves	☐ complete my tasks
☐ take inventory	☐ come to work on time
☐ solve problems	

B **Think about your job skills and personal traits. Check [✓] the information about you.
Then add your own information.**

My Skills and Personal Traits	
☐ I can work with machines.	☐ I can work with people.
☐ I can use a computer.	☐ I can solve problems.
☐ I can use a cash register.	☐ I can come to work on time.
☐ I can _____.	☐ I am responsible.
	☐ I am _____.

C **PAIRS** **Talk about your job skills and personal traits. Use the information in Exercise B.**

A: Please tell me about yourself.

B: I can _____, and I'm _____.
What about you?

A: I can _____, and I'm _____.

PUT YOUR IDEAS TO WORK

GROUPS Choose a job. Think about the job skills and personal traits you
need for that job. Make a list. Then share the list with the group.

GRAMMAR

In this unit, you studied:

- *Be:* Simple present negative statements
- *Be:* Simple present *yes / no* questions

See page 146 for your Grammar Review.

VOCABULARY See page 156 for the Unit 2 Vocabulary.

Vocabulary Learning Strategy: Use your first language

A Choose 10 words. In your notebook, write the word in English and in your first language.

B Underline 5 words from Exercise A. Write a sentence with each word on a separate piece of paper.

SPELLING See page 156 for the Unit 2 Vocabulary.

CLASS Choose 10 words for a spelling test.

LISTENING PLUS

A Watch each video. Write the story of Carmen's day on a separate piece of paper.

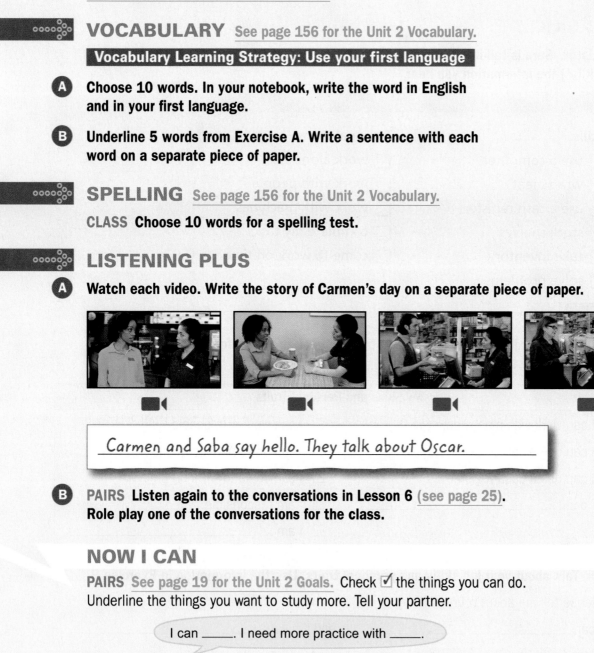

Carmen and Saba say hello. They talk about Oscar.

B **PAIRS** Listen again to the conversations in Lesson 6 (see page 25). Role play one of the conversations for the class.

NOW I CAN

PAIRS See page 19 for the Unit 2 Goals. Check ☑ the things you can do. Underline the things you want to study more. Tell your partner.

> I can _____. I need more practice with _____.

3 Oscar Is in Charge

MY GOALS

- ☐ Say goodbye
- ☐ Read traffic signs
- ☐ Ask for help
- ☐ Read a supermarket flyer
- ☐ Express likes and dislikes
- ☐ Read and say the time
- ☐ Ask permission to leave work early
- ☐ Look at job ads online

Go to MyEnglishLab for more practice after each lesson.

Oscar Perez

Oscar   *Today*
As a manager, I'm in charge of many things—and people! I have a lot of responsibility.

33

1 Say goodbye

GET READY

Oscar says there's terrible traffic.
How do you feel when you are in traffic?

WATCH

■◄ Watch the video. Read the sentences.
Circle *True* or *False*. Then correct the false sentences.

1. Oscar is at home.   True   False

2. The time is 7:10.   True   False

3. Oscar is late.   True   False

CONVERSATION

A ■◄ **Watch part of the video.**
Complete the conversation.

Oscar: I'll see you later. I've got to run now.

Isabel: Oh, wait, before you go . . . can you
get milk on the way home today?

Oscar: Um hmm.

Isabel: Thanks. Oh, hang on.
We also need bread.

Oscar: Yes, I'll get it. I have to go now.

Isabel: Sure. I'll call you later. _____.
                                          ★

Oscar: _____.
              ★★

> ### Pronunciation Note
>
> We stress important words in a sentence.
> We stress verbs, nouns, adverbs, and
> adjectives. Stressed words are long and loud.
>
> ◀)) **Listen and repeat.**
>   ●   ●
> **Drive care**fully.
>   ●   ●
> I'll **call** you **la**ter.
>   ● ●   ●
> There's a **bad ac**cident on the **high**way.

B ◀)) **Listen and repeat.**

C PAIRS **Practice the conversation.**

D PAIRS **Practice the conversation again.**
Use different ways to say *goodbye*.

WHAT DO YOU THINK?

GROUPS What do you do when there is a lot of traffic on your way to work or school?

PRACTICAL SKILLS

Read traffic signs

GET READY

What traffic signs do you see on your way to English class or to work?

TRAFFIC SIGNS

A ◀))) **Listen and look at the signs on the map.**
Listen and repeat.

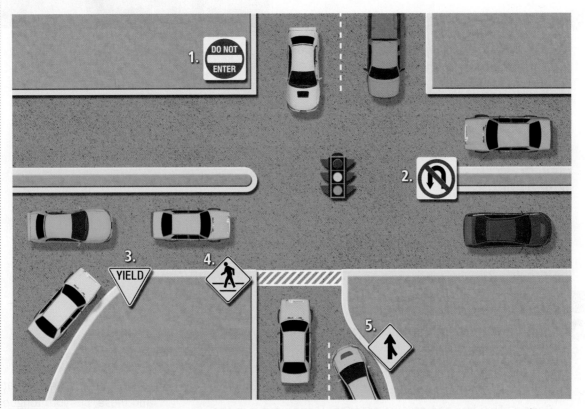

B **Read the sentences. Which sign matches the information?**
Write the number.

1. Move to the lane on your left.   _5_

2. Do not drive here.   ___

3. Go slow. Let other cars go first.   ___

4. Watch out. People are crossing here.   ___

5. Do not turn around in the street.   ___

> **Speaking Note**
>
> Ask for directions by saying:
> *Excuse me. Can you give me*
> *directions to . . . ?*

WHAT DO YOU THINK?

GROUPS On many highways in the U.S., the speed limit is
55 miles per hour. Do you think this is a safe speed limit?
Why or why not?

> I think 55 miles per hour
> is safe, because . . .

LISTENING AND SPEAKING

Ask for help

GET READY

Look at the picture. Oscar asks Wen for help.
When do you ask for help?

WATCH

**◼◀ Watch the video. Read the sentences.
Circle the correct answers.**

1. Oscar asks Wen for _____.
   a. oranges   **b.** help   **c.** organic produce

2. Oscar needs Wen to _____ a few boxes.
   a. pack   **b.** hand   **c.** unload

3. The boxes have _____.
   a. oranges   **b.** melons   **c.** broccoli

4. Wen needs to move the shopping cart to the _____ of the store.
   a. front   **b.** left   **c.** back

CONVERSATION

Ⓐ ◼◀ Watch part of the video. Complete the conversation.

Oscar: Can you help me _____ these boxes?
                                    ★

Wen: _____. Where do you want them?
                    ★★

Oscar: This box has organic oranges. Please put it in the organic section.

Wen: OK. What else do you need help with?

Oscar: Can you take those boxes to the back? Thanks, Wen.

Ⓑ ◀))) Listen and repeat.

Ⓒ PAIRS Practice the conversation. Use your own names.

**Ⓓ PAIRS Practice the conversation again.
Use different actions and different ways to say yes.**

> **Pronunciation Note**
>
> To say the *th* sound in *that* and *these*, put your tongue between your teeth. Use your voice to make this sound.
>
> **◀))) Listen and repeat.**
>
> this   that
> these   those
> there

WHAT DO YOU THINK?

PAIRS Saba works in customer service. She helps people and answers questions.
Think about other places where people work. Name jobs that involve helping people.

STUDY *This, that, these, those*

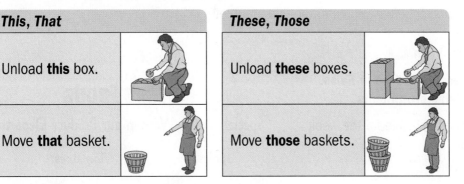

This, That	
Unload **this** box.	
Move **that** basket.	

These, Those	
Unload **these** boxes.	
Move **those** baskets.	

PRACTICE

A **Customers are asking for help. Underline the correct words.**

1. Can you help me with <u>this</u> / these shopping cart?

2. Can you get that / those boxes for me?

3. Can I use this / these phone?

4. Can you carry this / these bags for me?

> **Grammar Note**
>
> Use *this* and *these* for things that are close to you; use *that* and *those* for things that are not close.

B **Look at the pictures. Complete the sentences with *this*, *that*, *these*, or *those*.**

1. A: I'll use ___*this*___ credit card.

    B: Thank you.

2. A: Are _____ oranges from Florida?

    B: Yes, they are.

3. A: I want to use _____ coupons.

    B: OK. You saved $3.35.

4. A: Is _____ lettuce on sale?

    B: Yes, it is.

WHAT ABOUT YOU?

GROUPS Bring in a photo of your family or friends and tell your classmates about the people in it.

> These are my brothers, Luis and Nelson.

> This is my friend, Amina.

5 Read a supermarket flyer

GET READY

Do you check prices before you go to the supermarket?

SUPERMARKET FLYERS

A **Read the flyer. Circle *True* or *False*. Correct the false statements.**

1. The flyer has specials for the week in the deli.

   True   False

2. Pineapples are $2.99.

   True   False

3. Tomatoes are on sale for $2.89/lb.

   True   False

4. You can buy two bags of carrots for $1.99.

   True   False

5. Sale prices start on Monday.

   True   False

B **PAIRS Imagine. You have $25.00 to buy fruits and vegetables. What do you want to buy? Make a list.**

Speaking Note

Ask about specials by saying:
Excuse me. Do you have any specials today?

If you can't hear the quantity, say:
How much? or *How many?*

Fresh Foods

Specials of the Week in our Produce Department

Pineapples
reg. $4.99
now $2.99

Tomatoes
reg. $2.89/lb.
now $2.49/lb.

Apples
reg. $1.49/lb.
now $1.29/lb

Peppers
reg. $1.00 each
now 2 for $1.00

Oranges
reg. 3 for $2.00
now 4 for $2.00

Carrots
$1.99/bag,
now buy one, get one free

Sale prices start Sunday.

WHAT DO YOU THINK?

GROUPS What are some other ways to find out about sales and specials at the supermarket or other stores?

You can look on the Internet . . .

LISTENING AND SPEAKING

Express likes and dislikes

GET READY

Look at the picture. Oscar and a customer talk about things they like and don't like to eat.
What are some things you like and don't like to eat?

WATCH

A ■◄ **Watch the video. Read the sentences. Circle *True* or *False*. Then correct the false sentences.**

1. The customer needs chili peppers.	True	False
2. The customer's family likes spicy food.	True	False
3. Oscar's children eat spicy food.	True	False
4. The customer cooks fish with peppers, onions, and garlic.	True	False

B ■◄ **Watch the video again. Circle the answer.**

Oscar says, "That sounds good!" He is talking about _____.

a. fish   **b.** yellow onions

CONVERSATION

A ■◄ **Watch part of the video. Complete the conversation.**

Customer: _____ some chili peppers.
                          ★

Oscar: OK. They're over here. These peppers are not hot. Those are hot.

Customer: I like hot peppers. But my family doesn't like anything spicy.

Oscar: I really like spicy food. My children don't.
Do you need anything else?

Customer: Yes. I need some onions.

Oscar: Sure. _____ onions are over there.
                          ★★

B ◄))) **Listen and repeat.**

C **PAIRS Practice the conversation.**

D **PAIRS Practice the conversation again.**
Use different words to explain your needs.

WHAT DO YOU THINK?

PAIRS Oscar's children don't like spicy food. What can Oscar and his wife do?

7 Simple present: Statements

STUDY Simple present: Statements

Affirmative Statements

I	like	
You	eat	
We	want	
They	need	
Tom	likes	spicy food.
He	eats	
Susan	wants	
She	needs	

Negative Statements

I		like	
You	don't	eat	
We		want	
They		need	
Tom		like	spicy food.
He	doesn't	eat	
Susan		want	
She		need	

Grammar Note

Affirmative verbs with *he*, *she*, or *it* end with an s.
She cooks Italian food, but he doesn't cook Italian food.

PRACTICE

A **Underline the correct words.**

1. He don't / <u>doesn't</u> like broccoli.

2. She eat / <u>eats</u> salty foods.

3. They <u>want</u> / wants mild peppers.

4. We <u>don't</u> / doesn't need bananas.

5. You <u>like</u> / likes fish.

6. I <u>don't</u> / doesn't need onions.

B **Carmen tells a friend about her family. Write the correct form of the verb.**

I ___*eat*___ dinner at home with my daughters. They _____ meat, but they
⎵⎵1. eat⎵⎵   2. like

_____ vegetables. My daughter Irma _____ Chinese food all of the time.
3. not / like   4. want

Sometimes my sister and her husband _____ with us. My sister _____,
5. eat   6. not / cook

so I _____ for us. We _____ Mexican food!
7. cook   8. love

WHAT ABOUT YOU?

PAIRS Take turns. Ask and answer questions about foods you like.

Do you like oranges?

Yes, I do.

Do you like onions?

No, I don't.

PRACTICAL SKILLS

Read and say the time

GET READY

What time do you go to English class?

TELL TIME

A ◀))) **Listen to each sentence. Write the time.**

1. Samid gets up

at _____.

2. Samid takes a shower

at _____.

3. Samid goes to work

at _____.

4. Samid eats lunch

from _____

to _____.

5. Samid comes home

at _____.

6. Samid goes to sleep

at _____.

B **PAIRS Take turns. Point to a clock. Say the time.**

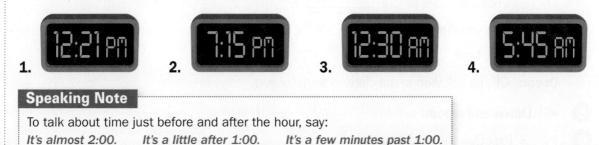

1. 2. 3. 4.

Speaking Note

To talk about time just before and after the hour, say:
It's almost 2:00.   *It's a little after 1:00.*   *It's a few minutes past 1:00.*

C **PAIRS Use the information in Exercise A. Tell your partner what you do each day. Say the time and use** A.M. **and** P.M.

WHAT DO YOU THINK?

GROUPS When do you study for your English class or for any other class?

LISTENING AND SPEAKING

9 Ask permission to leave work early

GET READY

Look at the picture. Joe asks to leave early.
What do you think Oscar is saying?

WATCH

A ■◄ **Watch the video. Was your guess correct?**

B ■◄ **Watch the video again. Put the sentences in order.**
Write 1, 2, 3, and 4.

_____ Oscar says he will ask Wen to work for Joe.

_____ Joe says he can stay until 4:00.

_____ Oscar asks Joe not to wait until same day to ask to leave early.

_____ Joe tells Oscar he needs to leave early.

C **Is Oscar happy with Joe? Explain your answer.**

_____

_____

CONVERSATION

A ■◄ **Watch part of the video. Complete the conversation.**

Joe: I need to leave early today.

Oscar: Today?

Joe: Yes. My car is at the garage.

           I need to leave before _____.
                                        ★

Oscar: Can you stay until _____?
                                   ★★

Joe: Yes, I can.

Oscar: OK. I'll ask Wen to stay late to work for you.

B ◄)) **Listen and repeat.**

C **PAIRS** **Practice the conversation.**

D **PAIRS** **Practice the conversation again. Use different times.**

WHAT DO YOU THINK?

GROUPS Joe leaves work early to pick up his car.
What reasons are OK to leave work early?
What reasons are not OK?

Write for a purpose

○○○○○○ **STUDY THE MODEL**

A **Read the email. Who is Joe writing to?**

Hi, Oscar,

I am writing because I need to leave work early on Wednesday. My car is in the garage and the garage closes at 6:00 P.M. I need to leave work at 4:45 P.M. Is this OK?

I can come in early tomorrow morning to make up the time.

Thank you.

Joe

B **Read the Writing Tip. Read the email again. Why is Joe writing the email? Write his purpose.**

_____

Writing Tip
The **purpose** is the reason you are writing. It tells the reader why you are writing.

○○○○○○ **BEFORE YOU WRITE**

PAIRS Imagine. You want to leave work early.
Answer these questions:

1. What is your reason for leaving early?

_____

2. Is your excuse OK?

_____

3. How do you think your boss will feel?

_____

4. Will you make up the time?

_____

○○○○○○ **WRITE**

Write to your boss. Say you need to leave early.
Give your reason. Study Joe's email and the Writing Tip.

Predict the topic: Look at pictures

GET READY

Read the Reading Skill. Look at the pictures. What do you see?
Guess. What do you think you will read about?

READD

◀))) **Listen and read the article. Was your guess correct?**

E-BIKES

Think about big cities in the world. There are a lot of cars, buses,
and taxis. This means there is a lot of traffic. It also means there
aren't enough parking spaces. There is also a lot of pollution.
Many people want to fix these problems.

One answer may be bicycles. Not regular bikes, but e-bikes.
E-bikes are electric bicycles. They look like a bicycle, but they
have an electric motor. They are small, so they are easy to park.
They don't use gas. Just plug your e-bike into a regular wall plug
and charge it each night.

E-bikes are already popular in Mumbai, Beijing, and London.
Now they are becoming more popular in New York, Los Angeles,
and São Paulo.

Will everyone use e-bikes? Some people say no. They think
older people will not use them. People living in places with a lot
of wet and cold weather will not use them. Also, some people
may be afraid to ride their e-bikes in traffic.

AFTER YOU READ

A Read the article again. Underline sentences or words
in the article that match the pictures.

B PAIRS Talk about your predictions and the pictures.
How did the pictures help you predict?

WHAT DO YOU THINK?

GROUPS Think about where you live now.
Do you think e-bikes are a good idea?
Why or why not?

Sara *Today*
I'm going to look online for a customer service representative job.

GET READY

Sara is looking for a job online. Have you ever looked for a job online?

ONLINE JOB ADS

 A Read the online job ads. Write the number of the ad that matches each place.

_____ restaurant   _____ supermarket

1.

Student • Professional • Opportunities • Counselors • Search

Customer Service Representative
Near public transportation
Part-time / Days
Apply online

Large supermarket looking for customer service representative. Must be a problem-solver. Must enjoy talking to customers. Cashier and computer skills required.

2.

Customer Care Representative

Are you good with customers? Can you work as a team with other employees? Join our restaurant team.

- must have customer service skills
- computer skills necessary
- full-time / weeknights and weekends
- must travel; need your own car

Apply online

B Read the job ads again. Write details about each job.

Details	Job 1	Job 2
Schedule	days	
PT / FT		
Skills		
Personal traits		
Transportation		
How to apply		

C **PAIRS** Think about a job you know. Write details. Then talk about the job.

Job: _____

Schedule: _____

Skills and personal traits needed: _____

Transportation: _____

PUT YOUR IDEAS TO WORK

GROUPS Look at the ads in Exercise A.
See page 17 and page 31.
Which job is better for Sara? Why?

I think job number _____ is better because _____.

GRAMMAR

In this unit, you studied:

- *This, that, these, those*
- Simple present: Statements

See page 147 for your Grammar Review.

VOCABULARY See page 157 for the Unit 3 Vocabulary.

Vocabulary Learning Strategy: Group words by part of speech

A Choose 8 nouns. Choose 8 verbs. Write them in 2 lists.

Nouns	Verbs	Nouns	Verbs
vegetable	carry		

B Underline 5 words from Exercise A. Write a sentence with each word on a separate piece of paper.

SPELLING See page 157 for the Unit 3 Vocabulary.

CLASS Choose 10 words for a spelling test.

LISTENING PLUS

A Watch each video. Write the story of Oscar's day on a separate piece of paper.

> Oscar is at work. He calls his wife, Isabel. He tells her that traffic is bad.

B **PAIRS** Review the conversation in Lesson 6 (see page 39).
Role play the conversation for the class.

NOW I CAN

PAIRS See page 33 for the Unit 3 Goals. Check ☑ the things you can do.
Underline the things you want to study more. Tell your partner.

> I can _____. I need more practice with _____.

4 Wen Likes his Job

MY GOALS

- ☐ Ask for something in a store
- ☐ Identify parts of the body
- ☐ Follow two-step instructions
- ☐ Talk about a favorite recipe
- ☐ Say days of the week
- ☐ Read a work schedule
- ☐ Talk about my work schedule

Go to MyEnglishLab for more practice after each lesson.

Wen Li

Wen *Today*
I like my job.
The best part of my job
is helping customers.

47

LISTENING AND SPEAKING

Ask for something in a store

GET READY

A customer needs help.
Guess. What do you think the customer asks Wen?

WATCH

A ■◀ **Watch the video.
Was your guess correct?**

B ■◀ **Watch the video again.
Read the sentences. Circle *True* or *False*.
Then correct the false sentences.**

1. A customer asks Wen for help.	True	False
2. The customer is looking for tomatoes.	True	False
3. Wen knows where the razor blades are.	True	False
4. The razor blades are in Aisle 10.	True	False
5. The shampoo is next to the soap.	True	False

CONVERSATION

A ■◀ **Watch part of the video. Complete the conversation.**

Customer: Where are the _____ ?
                             ★

Wen: They're in Aisle _____ .
                         ★★

Customer: Oh, OK. Thanks.

Wen: Do you need anything else?

Customer: Yes. Where is the shampoo?

Wen: It's in Aisle 11.

Customer: Aisle 11. Got it. Thanks for your help.

B ◀)) **Listen and repeat.**

C **PAIRS Practice the conversation.**

D **PAIRS Practice the conversation again.
Use different products and aisle numbers.**

WHAT DO YOU THINK?

PAIRS Wen works in the produce department. Customers often ask for help.
What should Wen do if he can't answer a customer's question?

2 *Be:* Simple present questions with *Where*

STUDY *Be:* Simple present questions with *Where*

Questions		
Where	**is**	the shampoo?
	are	the razor blades?

Answers	
It's	in Aisle 11.
They're	in Aisle 12.

Grammar Note

Write: *Where is.*
Say: *Where's.*

A **Complete the questions. Use *is* or *are*.**

1. Where _____*are*_____ the razors?

2. Where _____ the shampoo?

3. Where _____ the diapers?

4. Where _____ the deodorant?

5. Where _____ the toothpaste?

6. Where _____ the paper towels?

B **Read Saba's conversations at the customer service desk. Write *is*, *are*, *it's*, or *they're*.**

1. **A:** Excuse me. Where _____*is*_____ the bread?

   B: _____ in Aisle 8.

2. **A:** Can you help me? Where _____ the frozen foods?

   B: _____ in Aisle 9.

3. **A:** Excuse me. Where _____ the dairy section?

   B: _____ next to the meat department.

4. **A:** Excuse me. Where _____ the rice?

   B: _____ in Aisle 3.

5. **A:** Can you help me? Where _____ the tissues?

   B: _____ in Aisle 7.

C ◀))) **Listen and check your answers. Then listen and repeat.**

WHAT ABOUT YOU?

PAIRS Imagine. You are in a supermarket. Take turns.
Ask questions with *Where is* and *Where are*. Say where things are.

Where is the juice?

It's in Aisle 2.

③ Identify parts of the body

How many parts of the body can you name?

PARTS OF THE BODY

Ⓐ 🔊 **Listen and point. Listen and repeat.**

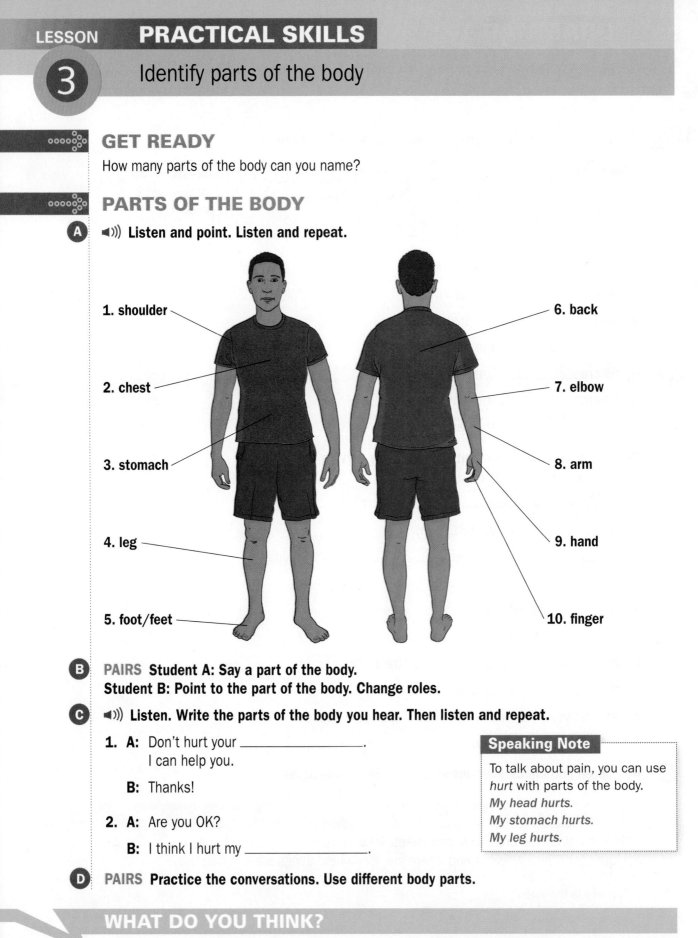

1. shoulder
2. chest
3. stomach
4. leg
5. foot/feet
6. back
7. elbow
8. arm
9. hand
10. finger

Ⓑ **PAIRS** Student A: Say a part of the body.
Student B: Point to the part of the body. Change roles.

Ⓒ 🔊 **Listen. Write the parts of the body you hear. Then listen and repeat.**

1. **A:** Don't hurt your _____.
I can help you.

   B: Thanks!

2. **A:** Are you OK?

   B: I think I hurt my _____.

> **Speaking Note**
>
> To talk about pain, you can use
> *hurt* with parts of the body.
> *My head hurts.*
> *My stomach hurts.*
> *My leg hurts.*

Ⓓ **PAIRS** **Practice the conversations. Use different body parts.**

WHAT DO YOU THINK?

PAIRS Talk about when you or someone you know gets hurt. What do you do?

GET READY

Look at the picture.

Guess. What happened?

WATCH

A ◼◀ **Watch the video.**
Was your guess correct?

B ◼◀ **Watch the video again.**
Read the sentences. Put the sentences in the correct order.
Write 1, 2, 3, or 4.

_____ Wen tells Joe to mop the floor.

_____ Wen sees the wet floor.

_____ Joe gets the warning signs.

_____ The customer spills coffee.

_____ The customer answers her phone.

CONVERSATION

A ◼◀ **Watch part of the video. Complete the conversation.**

Wen: Someone spilled coffee over here.

Joe: You're right. Look, it's over here, too.

Wen: Mop the floor, please. And make sure to put up some warning signs.

Joe: Right. I'll _____ the mop.
　　　　　　　　　★

Wen: And don't forget the signs. I'll wait here. We don't want

　　　　 anyone to _____.
　　　　　　　　　　　　　　★★

Joe: OK. I won't forget. I'll be right back!

B ◀)) **Listen and repeat.**

C **PAIRS** **Practice the conversation.**

D **PAIRS** **Practice the conversation again. Use different words.**

WHAT DO YOU THINK?

GROUPS Imagine. A customer falls and gets hurt. What should Wen do?

5 Talk about a favorite recipe

GET READY

Carmen talks about her grandmother's recipe for bean soup. Do you have any special family recipes?

WATCH

■◀ **Watch the video. Read the sentences. Circle** *True* **or** *False.* **Then correct the false sentences.**

1.	Wen says the soup smells good.	True	False
2.	The soup is spicy vegetable soup.	True	False
3.	Carmen says it's her mother's recipe.	True	False
4.	Carmen's children don't like this soup.	True	False
5.	The soup is easy to make.	True	False
6.	Carmen doesn't want to share the recipe.	True	False

CONVERSATION

A ■◀ **Watch part of the video. Complete the conversation.**

Wen: That smells _____. What is it?
⭐

Carmen: Spicy bean soup. It's my grandmother's recipe. Would you like to try some?

Wen: Sure. It's delicious! Can I have the recipe?

Carmen: Sure. You need black beans, two _____ yellow
⭐⭐
onions, one sweet red pepper, and tomatoes.

B ◀))) **Listen and repeat.**

C **PAIRS Practice the conversation.**

D **PAIRS Practice the conversation again. Use different adjectives.**

Pronunciation Note

Many English words begin with two consonant sounds. Say the sounds together.

◀))) **Listen and repeat.**

<u>sp</u>icy	<u>sm</u>all
<u>bl</u>ack	<u>fr</u>esh
<u>sw</u>eet	<u>sm</u>ells
<u>tr</u>y	<u>gr</u>andmother

WHAT DO YOU THINK?

GROUPS Imagine. You are invited to a friend's house. The food is spicy. But you don't like spicy food. What can you do?

> You can eat just a little bit of food . . .

GRAMMAR

Descriptive adjectives

STUDY Descriptive adjectives

Adjectives	Nouns	
yellow	onion	I need a **yellow onion** to make the soup.
spicy	peppers	Carmen put two **spicy peppers** in the soup.

> **Grammar Note**
>
> An adjective describes how something looks, feels, sounds, tastes, or smells.

PRACTICE

A Complete the sentences about Truda.
Choose adjectives and nouns from the box.
Write them in the correct order.

~~big~~	good	young
friendly	new	

children	people	~~supermarket~~
employee	schedule	

Truda works at a ___big___ ___supermarket___. She is a _____
                       1.   2.

_____. She works with many _____ _____.
                                                                             3.

Truda has a _____ _____. She works Monday to Friday.
                    4.

She spends the weekend with her two _____ _____.
                                                              5.

B Make sentences. Use the correct adjective and noun order.

1. ___I need a full-time job.___
                               need / job / a full-time / I

2. _____
                        in a busy / Oscar / department / works

3. _____
                        traffic today / heavy / there is

4. _____
                        yellow / needs / onions / Sara

5. _____
                        want / they / a different / schedule

6. _____
                        a new / manager / he is

WHAT ABOUT YOU?

PAIRS Write a list of six things you want buy at the supermarket.
For each thing, use an adjective and a noun. Then tell your partner.

> I need green grapes,
> two small onions, . . .

PRACTICAL SKILLS

7

Say days of the week

○○○○○○○ **GET READY**

Do you study English on a weekday or on the weekend?

DAYS OF THE WEEK

A ◀))) **Listen and point. Listen and repeat.**

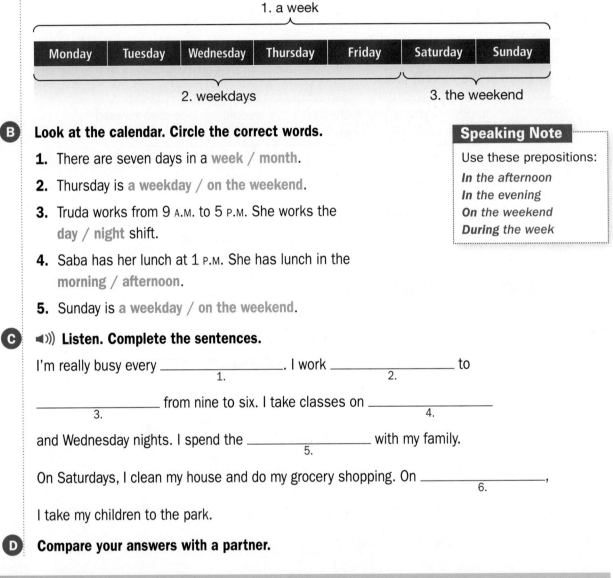

1. a week

| Monday | Tuesday | Wednesday | Thursday | Friday | Saturday | Sunday |

2. weekdays   3. the weekend

B **Look at the calendar. Circle the correct words.**

1. There are seven days in a week / month.

2. Thursday is a weekday / on the weekend.

3. Truda works from 9 A.M. to 5 P.M. She works the day / night shift.

4. Saba has her lunch at 1 P.M. She has lunch in the morning / afternoon.

5. Sunday is a weekday / on the weekend.

> **Speaking Note**
>
> Use these prepositions:
>
> *In* the afternoon
> *In* the evening
> *On* the weekend
> *During* the week

C ◀))) **Listen. Complete the sentences.**

I'm really busy every _____. I work _____ to
                              1.   2.

_____ from nine to six. I take classes on _____
          3.   4.

and Wednesday nights. I spend the _____ with my family.
                                          5.

On Saturdays, I clean my house and do my grocery shopping. On _____,
                                                                      6.

I take my children to the park.

D **Compare your answers with a partner.**

WHAT DO YOU THINK?

PAIRS Take turns. Tell your partner about your typical week.

I take my kids to school at 8:00 A.M.

I take a shower every day at 6:30 A.M.

Read a work schedule

GET READY

What kind of information can you find on a work schedule?

WORK SCHEDULES

A **Read the schedules. Answer the questions below.**

Produce Manager: Oscar Perez   Employee: Wen Li
Schedule: August 23–29

Sunday	Monday	Tuesday	Wednesday	Thursday	Friday	Saturday
	8:30 A.M.–3:30 P.M.	9:00 P.M.–4:00 A.M.		7:00 A.M.–3:00 P.M.	9:00 A.M.–4:00 P.M.	8:30 A.M.–3:30 P.M.

Deli Manager: Jim Robbins   Employee: Truda Mazur
Schedule: August 23–29

Sunday	Monday	Tuesday	Wednesday	Thursday	Friday	Saturday
	7:00 A.M.–3:00 P.M.	10:00 A.M.–3:00 P.M.	7:00 A.M.–3:00 P.M.	10:00 A.M.–3:00 P.M.		

Customer Service Manager: Layla Mohammed   Employee: Carmen Vasquez
Schedule: August 23–29

Sunday	Monday	Tuesday	Wednesday	Thursday	Friday	Saturday
10:00 A.M.–3:00 P.M.		10:00 A.M.–3:00 P.M.		10:00 A.M.–3:00 P.M.		10:00 A.M.–3:00 P.M.

1. Who is the deli manager? _____

2. Who works a night shift? _____

3. Who works only day shifts? _____

4. Who works on weekends? _____

5. Who works four days a week? _____

6. Who has one day off on the weekend? _____

> **Speaking Note**
>
> To ask about schedules, say:
> *When do you work?*
> *When are you off?*
> *When are you free?*
>
> To answer, say:
> *I work the day shift.*
> *I work the night shift.*

B **Write your schedule for this week. Then share your information with a classmate.**

WHAT DO YOU THINK?

PAIRS Think about your life now.
Describe the best work schedule for you.

> I go to school at night, so I need to work during the day . . .

LISTENING AND SPEAKING

Talk about your work schedule

GET READY

Wen and Truda talk about their work schedules.
What is your work or class schedule?

WATCH

■◀ **Watch the video. Read the sentences. Circle the correct answers.**

1. Truda works _____.
   a. on weekends   **b.** on weekdays   **c.** in the evening

2. Wen works on _____.
   a. Saturday   **b.** Sunday   **c.** Wednesday

3. Truda spends time with her _____ on the weekends.
   a. friends   **b.** family   **c.** coworkers

4. Wen likes to see _____ on the weekend.
   a. his friends   **b.** the movies   **c.** a menu

CONVERSATION

A ■◀ **Watch part of the video. Complete the conversation.**

Wen: Do you always work the _____ shift?
                                          ★

Truda: Yes. What about you?

Wen: I work some day shifts and some night shifts.

Truda: Do you work _____?
                                 ★★

Wen: Yes, but I'm off on _____.
                                    ★★

B ◀)) **Listen and repeat.**

C PAIRS **Practice the conversation.**

D PAIRS **Practice the conversation again. Use different shifts and days of the week.**

> **Pronunciation Note**
>
> *Do* often has a short, quiet pronunciation in questions. We often pronounce *do you* "d'ya."
>
> ◀)) **Listen and repeat.**
> Do you always work the day shift?
> Do you work weekends?

WHAT DO YOU THINK?

PAIRS A friend invites Wen to a party on Saturday night.
Wen wants to go, but he is on the schedule for that night. What can he do?

> He can tell his friend that he
> can't come to the party . . .

Predict the topic: Read headings

GET READY

Read the headings in the article. Guess.
What topic will you read about?

READD

🔊 **Listen and read the article.
Was your guess correct?**

ARE YOU SLEEPING ENOUGH?

We get up early to go to work. We stay up late to study or to have fun. Sometimes we feel stress and can't sleep. Is it a problem when we don't sleep? Is sleep important?

What happens when we don't sleep?
Not enough sleep can make you feel bad. It can make you gain weight. It can cause health problems like diabetes and high blood pressure. When people are tired, they can't pay attention well. They can have accidents. They also can't learn and remember information well.

Why is sleep important?
Sleep helps your body in many ways. It helps your body control blood pressure and fight illnesses. It improves memory.

How can you sleep better?
To sleep well, exercise every day. Keep your bedroom dark, quiet, and cool.

Try to go to bed and wake up at the same time every day. Don't drink coffee or soda before you sleep. Don't eat later than two to three hours before sleeping.

Remember, your body needs sleep to get ready for the next day or night! Sleeping longer will help you look younger, feel better, and live longer.

Hours of sleep needed each day	
Young children	11–13
Older children	10–11
Adults	7–9

AFTER YOU READ

Complete the sentence. Look at the chart.

Children aged 13 need this many hours of sleep: _____

WHAT ABOUT YOU?

GROUPS Tell the group about yourself. Do you get enough sleep?
What do you do to help you sleep?

Use correct tone

STUDY THE MODEL

A **Read Wen's email to Oscar. Why does Wen write this email?**

Dear Oscar:

I am writing to ask for a day off. My sister is getting married. The wedding is next Saturday.

I am on the schedule from 8:30 A.M. to 2:00 P.M. next Saturday. Can I change my schedule? I talked to Joe. He can work my shift on Saturday.

Please tell me if this change is OK.

Thank you very much.

Wen

B **Read the email again. Underline the polite words and phrases Wen uses.**

BEFORE YOU WRITE

PAIRS Imagine. You want to ask for a day off from work. Answer these questions:

1. Why do you want to take a day off? Give a reason.

_____

2. What date do you need to take off?

_____

3. Who can work for you?

_____

> **Writing Tip**
>
> When you write, think about the person to whom you are writing. Use the right **tone** (language) for that person. Use polite language for business.

WRITE

Write to your boss on a separate piece of paper. Ask to take a day off. Write your answers. Use polite language. Study Wen's email and the Writing Tip.

JOB-SEEKING SKILLS

Look at job ads in the newspaper

Sara *Today*
I'm going to look at job ads in the newspaper. Maybe I can find the job that Truda told me about.

GET READY

Sara is looking at job ads in the newspaper. Have you looked for jobs in newspapers? Which newspapers?

NEWSPAPER JOB ADS

A Look at the ads in the newspaper. Write the ad that matches each place.

_____ supermarket   _____ hospital

1.

> **Customer Service Associate**
> Are you a team player?
> Join our hospital group.
> <u>Exp req</u> with computers and customer service. FT. Nights & wknds. Refs req. Apply in person
> 17 Broadway

2.

> **Customer Service Representative**
> Supermarket needs Customer Service Rep PT M–F. Solve problems. Exp req with cash register and computers. All shifts available. Call for an interview, 703-555-6231

B Read the ads. Underline the abbreviations in each ad. Then write the abbreviations next to the full words.

1. _____exp req_____ experience required

2. _____ full time

3. _____ weekends

4. _____ references

5. _____ part time

6. _____ Monday to Friday

C Read the ads again. Match the job ads with the sentences.

1. The job is full time. _____1_____

2. You need experience with computers. _____

3. You need to be a problem-solver. _____

4. The job is for nights and weekends. _____

5. You need to give a reference letter. _____

6. You need to apply in person. _____

7. The job is Monday to Friday. _____

8. You need experience with a cash register. _____

PUT YOUR IDEAS TO WORK

GROUPS Look at the newspaper job ads in Exercise A. See page 17 and page 31. Which job is better for Sara? Why?

> I think job ad number _____ is better because _____.

GRAMMAR

In this unit, you studied:

- *Be:* Simple present questions with *Where*
- Descriptive Adjectives

See page 148 for your Grammar Review.

VOCABULARY See page 157 for the Unit 4 Vocabulary.

Vocabulary Learning Strategy: Recognize collocations

A Find words that are used together. Write them in a list.

Razor blades   Wet floor

B Underline 5 collocations in Exercise A. Write a sentence with each one on a separate piece of paper.

SPELLING See page 157 for the Unit 4 Vocabulary.

CLASS Choose 10 words for a spelling test.

LISTENING PLUS

A Watch each video. Write the story of Wen's day on a separate piece of paper.

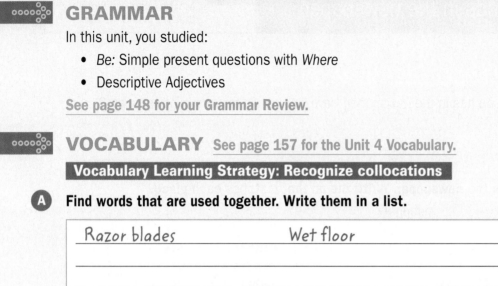

A customer asks Wen a question. Wen tells him where to find the razor blades.

B **PAIRS** Review the conversation in Lesson 4 (see page 51). Role play the conversation for the class.

NOW I CAN

PAIRS See page 47 for the Unit 4 Goals. Check ☑ the things you can do. Underline the things you want to study more. Tell your partner.

I can _____. I need more practice with _____.

5 Saba Doesn't Feel Well

MY GOALS

☐ Talk about the weather

☐ Say how I feel

☐ Identify months of the year

☐ Say and write dates

☐ Make a medical appointment

☐ Read an appointment card

☐ Confirm personal information

Go to MyEnglishLab for more practice after each lesson.

Saba Andarge

Saba   *Today*

I think I'm getting sick. I need to see the doctor.

61

1

Talk about the weather

GET READY

What is the weather like today where you are?

WATCH

◼◀ **Watch the video. Read the sentences.**
Circle *True* or *False*. Then correct the false sentences.

1.	The customer asks for a job application.	True	False
2.	It's cold and raining.	True	False
3.	Saba likes the weather.	True	False
4.	Tomorrow the weather will be the same.	True	False
5.	Saba has the weekend off.	True	False
6.	It is spring.	True	False

CONVERSATION

A ◼◀ **Watch part of the video. Complete the conversation.**

Customer: It's _____ this morning.
                                    ★

Saba: Yes. And it's _____ again! I'm not happy about it.
                                    ★★

Customer: The weather forecast for tomorrow is the same.

Saba: Oh, no. I hope the weekend is nice. I have Saturday and Sunday off!

Customer: It's spring. The weather should be nice!

B ◀))) **Listen and repeat.**

C **PAIRS** Practice the conversation.

D **PAIRS** Practice the conversation again.
Use different kinds of weather.

WHAT DO YOU THINK?

GROUPS Think about the seasons in your country.
What is the weather like for each season?

Say how you feel

GET READY

Wen hurt himself.

Guess. What is he looking for?

WATCH

A ◼◀ **Watch the video. Was your guess correct?**

B ◼◀ **Watch the video again. Read the sentences. Circle the correct answers.**

1. Wen has a _____.

   a. cough   **b.** cut   **c.** headache

2. Saba's _____ hurts.

   a. throat   **b.** back   **c.** nose

3. Carmen has _____.

   a. a stomachache **b.** a headache   **c.** the flu

4. Joe has a headache and _____.

   a. a stomachache **b.** a cough   **c.** the flu

CONVERSATION

A ◼◀ **Watch part of the video. Complete the conversation.**

Wen: How are you?

Saba: I don't feel well. I think I'm sick.

Wen: Oh, no. What's wrong?

Saba: I have a _____. And I'm really tired.
                              ★

Wen: Does your _____ hurt?
                          ★★

Saba: Yes, it does.

B ◀)) **Listen and repeat.**

C PAIRS **Practice the conversation.**

D PAIRS **Practice the conversation again. Use different symptoms and parts of the body.**

> **Pronunciation Note**
>
> In some questions and statements, the voice goes down at the end.
>
> ◀)) **Listen and repeat.**
>
> How are **you**?
>
> I don't **feel** well.
>
> What's **wrong**?
>
> I have a **cough**.

WHAT DO YOU THINK?

GROUPS Joe is sick. Oscar asks Wen to work Joe's shift. But Wen has plans with friends. What should he do?

> I think Wen should . . .

GRAMMAR

Simple present yes / no questions: *Have, hurt*

STUDY Simple present yes / no questions: *Have, hurt*

Yes / No questions: *Have*

Do	you		
Does	he she Saba	**have**	the flu?

Short answers

Yes,	I he she	do. does.	No,	I he she	don't doesn't.

Yes / No questions: *Hurt*

Does	your his her Saba's	throat	**hurt?**

Short answers

Yes,	it	does.	No,	it	doesn't.

> **Grammar Note**
>
> A long answer gives more information.
> *Yes, his throat hurts badly.*

A **Complete the sentences. Circle the correct answers.**

1. Do / (Does) Carmen have the flu?

2. Do / Does you have a doctor's appointment?

3. Do / Does his head hurt?

4. Do / Does he have a cut?

5. Do / Does we have bandages?

6. Do / Does your chest hurt?

B **Complete the conversations. Write *do, does, don't,* or *doesn't.***

1. **A:** _____Does_____ Saba have a cough?

   B: Yes, she _____does_____.

2. **A:** _____ Oscar and his wife have a cold?

   B: No, they _____.

3. **A:** _____ Joe's stomach hurt?

   B: No, it _____.

4. **A:** _____ you have a fever?

   B: Yes, I _____.

C ◀))) **Listen and check your answers. Then practice the conversations with a partner.**

WHAT ABOUT YOU?

PAIRS **Student A:** Ask your partner questions.
Student B: Give short and long answers. Then switch roles.

Do you have a fever?

No, I don't.

Does your head hurt?

Yes, all of the time.

PRACTICAL SKILLS

4 Identify months of the year

GET READY
Cover the calendars below. How many months of the year can you name?

MONTHS OF THE YEAR

A ◀))) **Listen and read. Listen and repeat.**

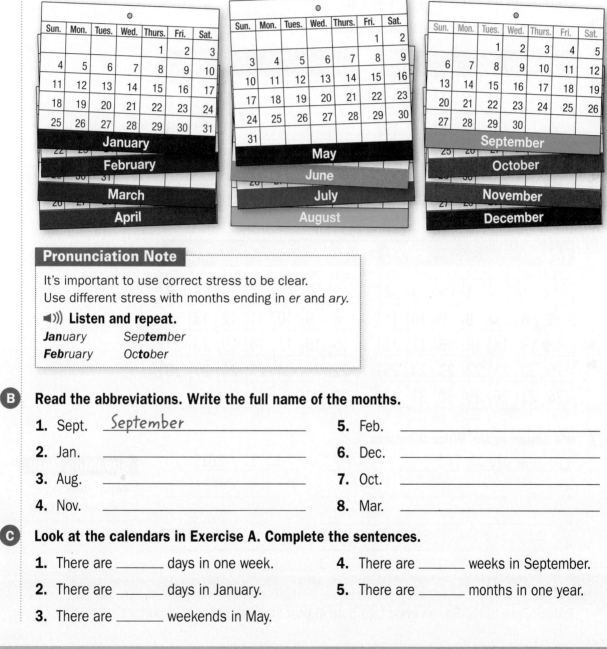

Pronunciation Note

It's important to use correct stress to be clear.
Use different stress with months ending in *er* and *ary*.

◀))) **Listen and repeat.**

| **Jan**uary | Sep**tem**ber |
| **Feb**ruary | Oc**to**ber |

B **Read the abbreviations. Write the full name of the months.**

1. Sept.   _September_
2. Jan.   _____
3. Aug.   _____
4. Nov.   _____

5. Feb.   _____
6. Dec.   _____
7. Oct.   _____
8. Mar.   _____

C **Look at the calendars in Exercise A. Complete the sentences.**

1. There are _____ days in one week.
2. There are _____ days in January.
3. There are _____ weekends in May.

4. There are _____ weeks in September.
5. There are _____ months in one year.

WHAT ABOUT YOU?

GROUPS What is your favorite month of the year? Why?

5 Say and write dates

GET READY

What is today's month and day?

ORDINALS AND DATES

A **PAIRS** Take turns. Say and write the names of the months.
Go to page 65 to check your spelling.

B ◀))) Listen and point. Listen and repeat.

January						2015
Sunday	Monday	Tuesday	Wednesday	Thursday	Friday	Saturday
				1	2	3
4	5	6	7	8	9	10
11	12	13	14	15	16	17
18	19	20	21	22	23	24
25	26	27	28	29	30	31

February						2016
Sunday	Monday	Tuesday	Wednesday	Thursday	Friday	Saturday
	1	2	3	4	5	6
7	8	9	10	11	12	13
14	15	16	17	18	19	20
21	22	23	24	25	26	27
28	29					

March						2017
Sunday	Monday	Tuesday	Wednesday	Thursday	Friday	Saturday
			1	2	3	4
5	6	7	8	9	10	11
12	13	14	15	16	17	18
19	20	21	22	23	24	25
26	27	28	29	30	31	

April						2018
Sunday	Monday	Tuesday	Wednesday	Thursday	Friday	Saturday
1	2	3	4	5	6	7
8	9	10	11	12	13	14
15	16	17	18	19	20	21
22	23	24	25	26	27	28
29	30					

C ◀))) Listen again. Write the dates.

1. January 21, 2015 _____ 1 / 21 / 2015 _____

2. _____ _____

3. _____ _____

4. _____ _____

> **Speaking Note**
> Write: *June 7.*
> Say: *June seventh.*

WHAT ABOUT YOU?

PAIRS Take turns. Say an important date in your life. Say why it is important.

On June 7, 1998, my son was born.

GET READY

Saba makes a phone call during her lunch break.
Guess. Who is she calling?

WATCH

A ▪◀ **Watch the video. Was your guess correct?**

B ▪◀ **Watch the video again. Circle the answer.**

1. Saba makes an appointment for _____.
   a. today   **b.** tomorrow

2. The receptionist asks Saba to spell _____.
   a. her first name   **b.** her last name

C **Read the statements about the video. Circle *True* or *False*.
Then correct the false statements.**

1. The doctor's office has an opening today.	True	False
2. Saba wants an earlier appointment.	True	False
3. Saba finishes work at 6:00.	True	False
4. The next appointment is tomorrow morning.	True	False

CONVERSATION

A ▪◀ **Watch part of the video. Complete the conversation.**

Receptionist: Hello. Arlington Clinic. Can I help you?

Saba: Hi. Do you have any appointments available today?

Receptionist: We have an opening at 1:00.

Saba: Is there a later appointment? I finish work at 4:00.

Receptionist: No, I'm sorry. I can give you tomorrow morning at _____.
                  ★

Saba: That's _____. I'll take it.
           ★★

B ◀))) **Listen and repeat.**

C **PAIRS Practice the conversation.**

D **PAIRS Practice the conversation again. Use different times and expressions.**

WHAT DO YOU THINK?

GROUPS Saba did not leave work early to see the doctor at 1:00.
When is it OK to leave work early?

LESSON 7 · PRACTICAL SKILLS

Read an appointment card

GET READY

What kinds of appointments do you make?

APPOINTMENT CARDS

A Read the card. Answer the questions.

Arlington Clinic
161 South Street / Arlington, VA 22304

Patient _Saba Andarge_

Doctor _Dr. Susi Li_

Date _April 24_

Time _9:30 A.M._

To cancel or change your appointment, please call
(703) 555-2851 one business day before your appointment.

> **Speaking Note**
>
> Ask for clarification by saying:
> *Excuse me. I can't read your writing. Can you print that?*

1. Who is the appointment for? _____

2. What date is the appointment? _____

3. What time is the appointment? _____

4. Who is Saba's doctor? _____

5. Saba needs to cancel. What number should she call? _____

B 🔊)) Listen to the telephone messages. Complete the appointment cards.

Arlington Clinic
161 South Street / Arlington, VA 22304

Patient _Robert Tan_

Doctor _Dr. Samuel Li_

Date _____

Time _____

Arlington Clinic
161 South Street / Arlington, VA 22304

Patient _Lisa Mason_

Doctor _Dr. Samuel Li_

Date _____

Time _____

C **PAIRS** Take turns. Choose a date and a time.
Call your partner and leave a message.

Hello. This is a message for _____.

This call is to confirm your appointment on _____ at _____.

Please call us if you need to cancel or change your appointment. Thank you.

WHAT DO YOU THINK?

GROUPS Some clinics ask you to change or cancel your appointment 24 hours before the appointment. If you don't, you have to pay. What do you think about this policy?

LISTENING AND SPEAKING

Make a medical appointment: Part 2

GET READY

The clinic receptionist asks Saba for some information. Guess. What questions do you think she will ask?

WATCH

A ◼◀ **Watch the video. Was your guess correct?**

B ◼◀ **Watch the video again. Complete the sentences. Use words from the box.**

> date   computer   contact   patient

1. The receptionist asks for Saba's _____ phone numbers.

2. Saba is not a new _____.

3. The receptionist confirms Saba's _____ of birth.

4. The office has a new _____ system.

CONVERSATION

A ◼◀ **Watch part of the video. Complete the conversation.**

Receptionist: What are your contact phone numbers?

Saba: My cell phone is 703-555-6735.

Receptionist: And your home phone?

Saba: 703-555-9419.

Receptionist: OK. And your date of birth is _____?
★

Saba: Correct.

Receptionist: Good. What is your current address?

Saba: It's 3725 South Washington Street, Apartment _____.
★★

B ◀))) **Listen and repeat.**

C **PAIRS** Practice the conversation.

D **PAIRS** Practice the conversation again. Use different dates and numbers.

Pronunciation Note

We pause (stop) a little between groups of numbers and words. We say the numbers or words in a group together.

◀))) **Listen and repeat.**

My cell phone / is 571- / 555- / 6735.

My home phone / is 571- / 555- / 9419.

My date of birth / is August 26, / 1982.

WHAT DO YOU THINK?

GROUPS Saba feels more comfortable with a woman doctor. What should she do when she calls to make an appointment?

> She should . . .

GRAMMAR

Be: Simple present questions with *What*

STUDY *Be:* **Simple present questions with *What***

What	is	your name? his work schedule?
	are	your home and work numbers? her hours on Sunday?

Speaking Note

You see: *What is*
You say: *What's*

A **Complete the sentences with *is* or *are*.**

1. What _____*is*_____ the problem?

2. What _____ your days off?

3. What _____ the weather forecast for tomorrow?

4. What _____ her address?

5. What _____ their hours next week?

B **Saba's husband has a new job.**
Write questions that he answers on forms.

1. _What is your ID number?_____
   your / is / ID number / what

2. _____
   home and cell phone numbers / are / what / your

3. _____
   what / email address / your / is

4. _____
   are / your / what / days off

5. _____
   date of birth / your / is / what

6. _____
   the names of / are / what / your family members

WHAT ABOUT YOU?

PAIRS Take turns. Ask and answer questions about favorite things.
Use *What is* or *What are.*

What are your favorite TV shows?

What is your favorite color?

My favorite TV shows are . . .

May favorite color is . . .

Skimming

GET READY

Skim the article. Do you want to read more?
Does it look interesting?

Reading Skill

To **skim an article** means to read the article quickly. Do not read every word. We skim an article to see what the topic is or to see if we want to read it.

READD

◀)) **Listen and read the article. Was your guess correct?**

JUST WALK IN

People usually go to a doctor or clinic when they are sick. They go to a supermarket to buy bread and milk. They go to a pharmacy for prescriptions. But now there are clinics in supermarkets and pharmacies.

These medical clinics are called *walk-in clinics*. They give medical help for sore throats, colds, and fevers. They are not expensive to visit.

There are walk-in clinics in many countries. For example, you can find them in England, India, Kenya, and the United States. Now there are more than 1,300 walk-in clinics in the U.S.

Why are more people going to walk-in clinics? They are easy to find. Many walk-in clinics are in busy shopping areas. They are open at night and on weekends. You don't need an appointment, either. Walk-in clinics are convenient, and that is important in today's busy world.

AFTER YOU READ

PAIRS What is the main idea of the article? Discuss and circle the best answer.

a. Walk-in clinics are growing around the world.

b. Walk-in clinics give help for sore throats, colds, and fevers.

c. Walk-in clinics are a new, inexpensive way to get medical help.

WHAT DO YOU THINK?

GROUPS Some people like walk-in clinics because they are convenient. They are not expensive. Some people like to go to the same doctor each time. What do you prefer?

I prefer to see a doctor.
I trust my doctor.
What do you prefer?

I prefer clinics because . . .

Give instructions

STUDY THE MODEL

Read the email from Saba's boss, Layla.
What does Saba need to read about?

a. meetings   **b.** paychecks   **c.** websites

Hi, Saba!

There is a meeting tomorrow morning about our new paychecks. I know you have a doctor's appointment. You can find the information you need on the store website.

1. First, go to the Fresh Foods website.

2. Next, click on *Employees*

3. Type in your user name. Then type your password.

4. Click on the link to *Paychecks.*

Please call Jim if you have questions.

I hope you feel better soon!

Layla

BEFORE YOU WRITE

Imagine you and your friend work at Fresh Foods. Your friend just moved. Tell her how to change her address on the company website. Look at the art. Write the steps.

Writing Tip

Write steps or instructions in the correct order. Use numbers or words such as *first, next,* and *then* to make the order clear.

1.

http://www.freshfoods.com

2. Employees

User name:
Password:

3.

4. Contact Information

WRITE

On a piece of paper, write the email with instructions. Use the Writing Tip.
Use *first, next, then.*

JOB-SEEKING SKILLS

Complete a job application: Part 1

Sara *Today*
I'm going to Fresh Foods today. I'm going to fill out an application for the customer service job.

GET READY

◀)) Listen. Sara is asking for a job application. What job is she interested in?

JOB APPLICATION: PART 1

A Read the job application. Did Sara fill it out correctly? What is missing?

Fedmart
Employment Application

Personal Information

Name _Sara Moreno_ Phone _703-555-4236_

Address _1469 Sherman Street_ City _Fairfax_ State _VA_ Zip Code _22030_

Are you 18 years of age or older? Yes _X_ No _____

When can you begin to work? _Immediately_

Are you interested in full-time? _____ Part-time? _✓_

Can you work overtime? Yes _____ No _✓_

	Sunday	Monday	Tuesday	Wednesday	Thursday	Friday	Saturday
From	X	9:00 A.M.	9:00 A.M.	9:00 A.M.	9:00 A.M.	9:00 A.M.	X
To	X	2:30 P.M.	2:30 P.M.	2:30 P.M.	2:30 P.M.	2:30 P.M.	X

Are you legally able to work in the US? Yes _✓_ No _____

B Read the application again. Answer the questions.

1. Where does Sara live? _____

2. When can Sara start to work? _____

3. Can Sara work overtime? _____

4. When can Sara work on Mondays? _____

5. When can't Sara work? _____

6. Can Sara work in the U.S.? _____

PUT YOUR IDEAS TO WORK

PAIRS See the job application on page 161. Complete the personal information section. Use your own or made up information. Show it to your partner.

GRAMMAR

In this unit, you studied:

- Simple present *yes / no* questions: *have, hurt*
- *Be:* Simple present questions with *What*

See page 149 for your Grammar Review.

VOCABULARY   See page 158 for the Unit 5 Vocabulary.

Vocabulary Learning Strategy: Write personal sentences

Write sentences about yourself using 7 of the words.

> Summer is my favorite season.
> My date of birth is August 23, 1990.

SPELLING   See page 158 for the Unit 5 Vocabulary.

CLASS Choose 10 words for a spelling test.

LISTENING PLUS

A Watch each video. Write the story of Saba's day on a separate piece of paper.

> Saba is at the Customer Service desk. She talks to a customer about the weather.

B PAIRS Review the message in Exercise C of Lesson 7 (see page 68). Role play the message for the class.

NOW I CAN

PAIRS See page 61 for the Unit 5 Goals. Check ☑ the things you can do.
Underline the things you want to study more. Tell your partner.

> I can _____. I need more practice with _____.

6 Saba Goes to the Doctor

MY GOALS

☐ Change an appointment

☐ Sign in at a medical office

☐ Follow medical instructions

☐ Talk about my symptoms

☐ Give and follow advice

☐ Read a medicine label and dosage

☐ Call in sick

Go to MyEnglishLab for more practice after each lesson.

Saba Andarge

Saba   *Today*

I need to take a sick day. I'm going to take some medicine and rest.

LISTENING AND SPEAKING

1 Change an appointment

GET READY

Saba needs to bring a form of identification to her medical appointment.

What forms of ID do you have?

WATCH

◼◀ **Watch the video. Read the sentences. Circle the correct answers.**

1. Saba calls the _____.
   a. supermarket   **b.** hospital   **c.** clinic

2. Saba changes her appointment to _____.
   a. 9:45   **b.** 10:45   **c.** 9:30

3. Saba needs to bring _____.
   a. a parking ticket   **b.** construction   **c.** ID

4. Saba needs to park on Level _____ of the garage.
   a. A   **b.** B   **c.** C

> **Pronunciation Note**
>
> Important words in a sentence are stressed. They are long and loud. Words like *a*, *an*, *for*, and *of* are usually short and quiet.
>
> ◀))) **Listen and repeat.**
>
> I may have an opening for later.
>
> Bring a form of ID.

CONVERSATION

A ◼◀ **Watch part of the video. Complete the conversation.**

Saba: I have an appointment today at 9:30, but I overslept. Can I please change my appointment?

Receptionist: Let me check. I may have an opening for later.

               Can you come in this morning at _____?
                                                    ★

Saba: Yes, I can. That's great.

Receptionist: Bring your insurance card and a form of ID, please.

Saba: Can I use my _____?
                                  ★★

Receptionist: Yes, you can.

B ◀))) **Listen and repeat.**

C **PAIRS** Practice the conversation.

D **PAIRS** Practice the conversation again. Use different times and kinds of ID.

WHAT DO YOU THINK?

GROUPS What kinds of medical clinics and doctor offices are in your neighborhood?

Imperatives

ooooo **STUDY** Imperatives

Affirmative	Negative
Park on Level B of the garage.	**Don't park** on Level A.

Grammar Note

Use *don't* or *do not* to form the negative imperative.
To be polite, use *please* before an imperative.

Please *give me your insurance card.*

ooooo **PRACTICE**

A Underline the correct forms.

1. Don't exercise / <u>Exercise</u> five times a week.

2. Don't close / Close the door. The teacher is coming in.

3. Don't eat / Eat fruits and vegetables to stay healthy.

4. Don't sleep / Sleep eight hours of sleep every day. You will feel much better!

5. Don't spill / Spill coffee on the floor, please.

6. Don't arrive / Arrive late. Your boss is waiting for you.

B Unscramble the words. Write affirmative and negative imperatives.

1. ID / your / bring   *Bring your ID.* _____

2. 15 / come / early / minutes   _____

3. park / of the street / on this side / don't   _____

4. out / fill / forms / the   _____

5. late / don't / be   _____

6. your / sign / name   _____

7. please / this way / come   _____

C ◄))) Listen and check your answers.

WHAT ABOUT YOU?

GROUPS One student gives commands. The other students do the actions.
Then change roles.

Sit over here.   Pick up your books.

GET READY

What do you do when you arrive for a doctor's appointment?

SIGN-IN SHEETS

Westside Medical Clinic
Sign-In Sheet for 6/21/2015

Patient Name	Appointment time	Arrival time	Doctor
1. Samantha Carter	8:15 A.M.	8:00 A.M.	Dr. Sam Li
2. Erdem Asker	8:45 A.M.	8:55 A.M.	Dr. Sam Li
3. Saba Andarge	10:45 a.m.	10:30 a.m.	Dr. Susi Park

A Read the sign-in sheet. Answer the questions.

1. What is the date on the sign-in sheet? _____

2. Who has the first appointment? _____

3. What time did Erdem Asker arrive? _____

4. What time is Saba's appointment? _____

5. Who arrived late today? _____

B ◄)) Listen. Patients are checking in. Write their information on the form.

> **Speaking Note**
>
> Ask for information by saying: *Excuse me....*

Westside Medical Clinic
Sign-In Sheet for 6/22/2015

Patient Name	Appointment time	Arrival time	Doctor
1. Sara Assam		10:10 A.M.	Dr. James Roy
2. Jasmine Trinh		1:00 P.M.	Dr. Sam Li
3. David Brown			Dr. James Roy

C PAIRS Who arrived early? Who arrived late?

ROLE PLAY

PAIRS **Student A:** You are the receptionist.
Student B: You are the patient.
Check in at the clinic. Then change roles.

GET READY

Think about the last time you had a doctor's appointment.
What instructions did the doctor give you?

MEDICAL INSTRUCTIONS

A ◀))) **Listen and point. Listen and repeat.**

1. Sit on the table.

2. Take a deep breath.

3. Open your mouth and say "Ahh."

4. Look straight ahead.

5. Hold out your arm.

6. Make a fist.

Speaking Note

If you don't understand say: *I'm sorry. Could you repeat that, please?*

B **PAIRS** **Student A:** You are the doctor. Give the medical instructions in Exercise A.
Student B: Follow the doctor's instructions.
Then change roles.

WHAT DO YOU THINK?

GROUPS Imagine. A patient doesn't understand the doctor's medical instructions.
What should he or she do?

5

Talk about your symptoms

GET READY

Saba is at the supermarket.

Guess. Why do you think she goes there after her doctor's appointment?

WATCH

A ▪◀ **Watch the video.
Was your guess correct?**

B ▪◀ **Watch the video again. Read the sentences.
Circle *True* or *False*. Then correct the false sentences.**

1.	Saba has a stomachache.	True	False
2.	Carmen doesn't feel well.	True	False
3.	Saba has a fever.	True	False
4.	Saba has a cough.	True	False
5.	Saba needs to take a sick day.	True	False

CONVERSATION

A ▪◀ **Watch part of the video. Complete the conversation.**

Carmen: You look _____ ★. Are you OK?

Saba: No. I have bronchitis.

Carmen: Bronchitis?

Saba: Yes. I have a fever, and my _____ ★★ hurts.

Carmen: I'm sorry you don't feel well. Vikram is sick, too.

Saba: What's wrong with him?

Carmen: He has a fever and chills.

B ◀))) **Listen and repeat.**

C **PAIRS** **Practice the conversation.**

D **PAIRS** **Practice the conversation again.
Use different symptoms and parts of the body.**

WHAT DO YOU THINK?

PAIRS Imagine. Saba goes to the clinic, but she doesn't understand what the doctor tells her. What can she do?

LISTENING AND SPEAKING

Follow advice when you are sick

GET READY

Carl is a pharmacist at Fresh Foods.
He helps people choose medicine.
What medicine do you take when you're sick?

WATCH

■◀ **Watch the video. Read the sentences.
Circle *True* or *False*. Then correct the false sentences.**

1. Saba needs to buy some cough medicine.   True   False

2. Saba wants to buy the tablets.   True   False

3. The 12-hour cough syrup is for the daytime.   True   False

4. The cough syrup will make Saba tired.   True   False

CONVERSATION

Ⓐ ■◀ **Watch part of the video. Complete the conversation.**

Carl: Try this. It's a multi-symptom cold medicine. It lasts 8 to 12 hours.

Saba: Will it make me _____⭐?

Carl: Yes. You should take it _____⭐⭐.

Saba: I will!

Carl: Don't take it during the day. Here's a different medicine for daytime.

Saba: OK.

Carl: This will stop your headache, too.

Saba: Oh, good!

Carl: Make sure to get a lot of rest, Saba. That's the most important thing.

Ⓑ ◀)) **Listen and repeat.**

Ⓒ **PAIRS Practice the conversation.**

Ⓓ **PAIRS Practice the conversation again. Use different ways
to say *tired* and different times of day.**

WHAT DO YOU THINK?

GROUPS Saba takes care of her friend's daughter on Saturdays.
Now she is sick. What should she do?

7 Read a medicine label and dosage

○○○○○○○
GET READY

Some people don't like to take medicine. What about you?

○○○○○○○
MEDICINE LABELS AND DOSAGES

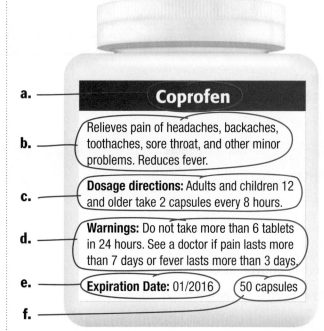

a.

b.

c.

d.

e.

f.

(A) **Read the medicine label. Write the letter that matches the information.**

_____ **1.** This is why I take this medicine.

_____ **2.** After this day, I shouldn't take this medicine.

_____ **3.** This tells me how many pills are in this bottle.

_____ **4.** This is important information, and I should be careful.

_____ **5.** This is how much medicine I should take.

_____ **6.** This is the name of the medicine.

(B) **Read the label again. Circle *Yes* or *No*.**

1. Carmen's seven-year-old daughter can take this medicine.   Yes   No

2. Saba should take this medicine at 7 A.M., 3 P.M., and 10 P.M.   Yes   No

3. Today is March 13, 2016. Saba can take this medicine.   Yes   No

WHAT DO YOU THINK?

GROUPS Younger children should take a different dosage of medicine than adults. Talk about the reasons why.

8

Call in sick

GET READY

Saba is calling Layla.

Guess. What is she going to say?

WATCH

A ◼◀ **Watch the video. Was your guess correct?**

B ◼◀ **Watch the video again. Read the sentences.**
Put them in order. Write 1, 2, 3, or 4.

_____ **a.** Layla will ask Saba's coworkers to take Saba's shifts.

_____ **b.** Saba needs to take two sick days.

_____ **c.** Saba will call Layla on Thursday.

_____ **d.** Saba calls Layla.

CONVERSATION

A ◼◀ **Watch part of the video. Complete the conversation.**

Layla: How are you? I was worried about you.

Saba: I'm sick. I have bronchitis.

Layla: Oh, no!

Saba: And the doctor says I shouldn't go to work

for _____ days.
⭐

Layla: OK. I'll find someone to take your shifts.

Saba: Thank you. I'm sorry about that.

Layla: Not at all. It's not your fault. You take care now.

You should _____ and drink tea.
⭐⭐

B ◀ᴗᴗ **Listen and repeat.**

C PAIRS **Practice the conversation.**

D PAIRS **Practice the conversation again. Use different words.**

> **Pronunciation Note**
>
> _Should_ usually has a short, quiet pronunciation: "sh'd." The negative _shouldn't_ is stressed and has a longer pronunciation.
>
> ◀ᴗᴗ **Listen and repeat.**
>
> You should **rest**.
>
> You should **drink tea**.
>
> I **should**n't **work** for **two days**.

WHAT DO YOU THINK?

GROUPS Many people don't stay home when they're sick.
What do you do when you're sick?

GRAMMAR

Should / Shouldn't

STUDY Should / Shouldn't

Affirmative Statements			
I You He She Saba We They	**should**	**stay**	home.

Negative Statements			
I You He She Saba We They	**shouldn't**	**stay**	home.

PRACTICE

A **Read the sentences. Circle the correct words.**

1. I (should) / shouldn't eat fruits and vegetables to stay healthy.

2. He should / shouldn't drink tea when his throat hurts.

3. We should / shouldn't sleep a lot when we have a cold.

4. They should / shouldn't go to school when they have a fever.

5. You should / shouldn't wash your hands if you are sick.

B **Complete the sentences. Write *should* or *shouldn't* and the correct form of the verb.**

Saba is sick. She _____*should stay*_____ home and rest.
　　　　　　　　　　　　　1. stay

She _____*shouldn't do*_____ too much.
　　　　　　2. not / do

The doctor says she _____ to work.
　　　　　　　　　　　　　　　3. not / go

She _____ tea.
　　　　　　4. drink

She _____ a pain reliever during the day.
　　　　　　　5. take

Saba's friends _____ too much.
　　　　　　　　　　　6. not / visit

She _____ her boss in two days.
　　　　　7. call

WHAT ABOUT YOU?

GROUPS What should and shouldn't you do when you are sick?
Make a list to share with the class.

> You should get a lot of rest.

> You shouldn't play sports.

Scanning

GET READY

Imagine. You have a cold. Read the article quickly.
Underline the information that will help you.

READ

◀))) **Listen and read the article. Circle other advice
that will help you to cure a cold.**

Reading Skill

To **scan an article** means to
look quickly at the article.
Look for the information you
want. Do not read every word.

KITCHEN CURES

Imagine. You wake up in
the morning. You have a
runny nose and a cough.
You are sneezing. You
feel very tired.

You probably have the common cold. It is
called the common cold because people
get colds all the time. Colds are not
dangerous. But a cold makes you feel bad.

Many people do not go to the doctor
when they have a cold. They use a home
remedy to feel better. A home remedy is
not medicine. It is something you do at
home to cure a problem like a cold. Maybe
you learned about the home remedy from
your mother or grandmother.

People often make home remedies with
fruits, drinks, or spices common in their
country. For example, in India, people
drink warm milk with honey, turmeric,
and ginger to help a cold. In Italy, people
say eating lots of garlic helps a cold. In
China, people use green tea with ginger
or honey.

In many countries, chicken soup is a
popular home remedy. Why do so many
people think it helps a cold? Scientists
have found that chicken soup helps the
body fight many cold symptoms. It clears
your throat and nose. But maybe chicken
soup makes us feel better because it is
made with love.

AFTER YOU READ

PAIRS Compare the advice you found. Did anything surprise you?

WHAT ABOUT YOU?

GROUPS Talk about home remedies from your family or your country.
Describe the remedy and what it helps.

11

Give advice

STUDY THE MODEL

A **Read the email. What's wrong with Saba?**

Hi, Saba.

Layla says you're sick. How are you feeling?

Can I give you some advice? I think you should stay home. Don't come to work. You need to rest and get better! Try to drink a lot of water and tea. My grandmother says it stops a cough. Chicken soup helps, too. It makes your body stronger. And remember, you need to sleep a lot. Sleep is very important. It helps your body fight the bronchitis.

I hope you feel better soon!

Truda

B **Read the Writing Tip. Then read Truda's email again. Underline the sentences with *should*, *need to*, and imperatives.**

> **Writing Tip**
>
> Use *should* to **write advice**.
> You can also use imperatives
> —for example, *Don't come to work.*

BEFORE YOU WRITE

PAIRS Imagine. Your friend is sick or hurt. What advice can you give him or her? How can he or she get better? Write your advice below.

_____

_____

_____

_____

WRITE

Write advice to your friend. Use *should* and imperatives.
Use your information from Before You Write.
Study Truda's email and the Writing Tip.

Sara *Today*
I'm going to fill out an online application at a kiosk at another supermarket.

GET READY

Sara is completing the education and work history sections of her job application. Have you ever completed a job application? Online?

JOB APPLICATION: PART 2

**Read the education and work history section of Sara's application.
Answer the questions.**

Most Recent Education

School Name: Mid-City Adult School   **Address:** 1300 Washington Blvd.

City: Fairfax   **State:** VA   **Zip Code:** 22030   **Phone Number:** (703) 555-4200

Courses: Adult High School Program, Bookkeeping courses

Highest Level of Education Completed: 12th Grade

Did you graduate high school? Yes ● **No** ◉ **GED Diploma** ◉

Work History (list your most recent job)

1. Company: Shoppers Market   **Phone #:** (703) 555-9020

Street: 403 Rose Avenue   **City:** Fairfax   **State:** VA   **Zip Code:** 22030

Job: Deli worker   **Supervisor:** Matt Peters

Dates Worked: June 2006 to April 2010   **Salary:** $10.00/hour

Reason for Leaving: left to have a baby and take care of my children

2. Company: Dollar Store   **Phone #:** (703) 555-6129

Street: 135 Bank Street   **City:** Fairfax   **State:** VA   **Zip Code:** 22030

Job: Cashier   **Supervisor:** Linda James

Dates Worked: January 2003 to May 2006   **Salary:** $7.75/hour

Reason for Leaving: wanted to earn more money and to work more hours

Have you served in the U.S. Military? Yes ◉ **No** ●

1. Where did Sara work from June 2006–April 2010? _____

2. What was Sara's most recent job? _____

3. Where did Sara make more per hour? _____

4. Why did Sara leave the Dollar Store? _____

5. Why did she leave Shoppers Market? _____

PUT YOUR IDEAS TO WORK

PAIRS Complete the education and work history section. See the job application on page 161. Use your own or made-up information. Show it to your partner.

GRAMMAR

In this unit, you studied:

- *Imperatives*
- *Should / Shouldn't*

See page 150 for your Grammar Review.

VOCABULARY See page 158 for the Unit 6 Vocabulary.

Vocabulary Learning Strategy: Group words by number of syllables

A Find words with 1, 2, or 3 syllables. Write them in the chart.

One Syllable	Two Syllables	Three Syllables
Rest	Toothache	Exhausted

B Underline 5 words from Exercise A. Write a sentence with each word on a separate piece of paper.

SPELLING See page 158 for the Unit 6 Vocabulary.

CLASS Choose 10 words for a spelling test.

LISTENING PLUS

A Watch each video. Write the story of Saba's day on a separate piece of paper.

Saba sleeps late. She calls the doctor's office.

B PAIRS Listen again to the conversations in Lesson 3 (see page 78).
Role play one of the conversations for the class.

NOW I CAN

PAIRS See page 75 for the Unit 6 Goals. Check ☑ the things you can do.
Underline the things you want to study more. Tell your partner.

I can _____. I need more practice with _____.

7 Oscar Wants to Move

MY GOALS

☐ Call about an apartment for rent

☐ Give an address

☐ Read an apartment ad

☐ Talk about moving to a new apartment

☐ Give directions

☐ Read a map

☐ Talk about my apartment

Go to MyEnglishLab for more practice after each lesson.

Oscar Perez

Oscar   *Today*
We need more space!
I'm going to look at
a bigger apartment.

1 Call about an apartment for rent

GET READY

Oscar wants to see an apartment.
He's calling the landlady.
Guess. What do you think Oscar will say?

WATCH

A ◼◀ **Watch the video. Was your guess correct?**

B ◼◀ **Watch the video again. Read the sentences. Circle the correct answers.**

1. Oscar is calling about _____.

    a. a house   **b.** a condominium   **c.** an apartment

2. Oscar is going to see the apartment _____.

    a. tonight   **b.** right now   **c.** tomorrow

3. The apartment is on _____ Street.

    a. Bond   **b.** Bank   **c.** Brick

CONVERSATION

A ◼◀ **Watch part of the video. Complete the conversation.**

Oscar: Hi. My name is Oscar Perez. I'm calling

about the _____ for rent.
                                 ★

Landlady: Yes, it's still available.

Oscar: Can I see it today?

Landlady: Well, the painters are working here now.

Oscar: How about tonight?

Landlady: Sure. Can you come around _____?
                                               ★★

Oscar: That's perfect.

B ◀))) **Listen and repeat.**

C **PAIRS** Practice the conversation again. Use your own name.
Use different homes and times.

> **Pronunciation Note**
>
> The vowel sound in a stressed syllable is long and clear: a**bout**.
> The vowel in other syllables is often short and quiet: about.
>
> ◀))) **Listen and repeat.**
> a•partment   a•vailable
> to•day   to•night

WHAT DO YOU THINK?

GROUPS Oscar and his wife have an appointment to see
the apartment tonight. What should Oscar and his wife do
if his parents can't watch the children?

> They should . . .

PRACTICAL SKILLS

2 Give an address

GET READY

When do you give your address?
Give examples.

ADDRESSES

A 🔊 **Listen and read the conversation. What is the address?**

A: What's your address, please?

B: 2679 North Shore Drive.

A: What's your apartment number?

B: Apartment 221.

A: What city?

B: Reston. R-E-S-T-O-N.

A: OK. And the state is Virginia . . . and your zip code?

B: 20190.

A: Thank you.

B **PAIRS** Practice the conversation.

C **PAIRS** Practice again. Use your own address or made-up information.

D Fill in the form. Use true or made-up information.

Fresh Foods Savings Card

First name   Last name

Street address

City   State   Zip code

Abbreviations
Road – Rd.
Avenue – Ave.
Street – St.
Drive – Dr.
Boulevard – Blvd.

WHAT DO YOU THINK?

GROUPS When is it a bad idea to give your address to someone?

GET READY

Have you looked for an apartment or house in the newspaper or on the Internet?
What happened?

APARTMENT ADS

www.findapartments.com

Apartment for rent on a quiet street

There are 3 bedrooms, 1 bathroom, a living room,
a dining room, and a new kitchen. Includes washer and
dryer and air conditioner. All utilities are included.

To make an appointment call 703-555-3746.

A Read the ad. Circle *True* or *False*. Then correct the false sentences.

1. There are two bedrooms.	True	False
2. There is one bathroom.	True	False
3. The kitchen is old.	True	False
4. The rent includes the utilities.	True	False

B Ads in newspapers use abbreviations. Match the words and abbreviations.

1. apartment
2. bedroom
3. living room
4. washer and dryer
5. utilities included

a. W/D
b. util. incl.
c. BR
d. LR
e. apt.

> **More abbreviations**
> bathroom – BA
> dining room – DR
> kitchen – Kit.

WHAT DO YOU THINK?

PAIRS Read the ads. Say which apartment you like and why.

Apartment A
Small apt, quiet street, 1 BR, 1 BA, LR, small eat-in K, air-conditioning, no W/D but laundry in basement. Call 703-555-8511.

Apartment B
Near stores, 2 BR, 2 BA, LR, DR, new kitchen, W/D, util not incl. Call 703-555-9215.

Talk about moving to a new apartment

GET READY

Oscar is looking for a new apartment.

Guess. Why do you think he and his family need a new apartment?

WATCH

A ■◀ **Watch the video. Was your guess correct?**

B ■◀ **Watch the video again. Read the sentences. Circle *True* or *False*. Then correct the false sentences.**

1.	Oscar is going to see a new apartment.	True	False
2.	Jim thinks the apartment is far from work.	True	False
3.	The apartment is far from Oscar's parents.	True	False
4.	Oscar is excited.	True	False

CONVERSATION

A ■◀ **Watch part of the video. Complete the conversation.**

Oscar: I'm going to see a new apartment after work.

Jim: Oh, yeah? Where is it?

Oscar: It's on Bank Street, close to Peter's Restaurant.

Jim: That's a _____ neighborhood, but it's far from work.
★

Oscar: I know, but it's close to my parents' apartment. We have two kids now, and they help us a lot.

Jim: Yeah, that's good. How do you feel about moving?

Oscar: I don't know. I'm worried.

The rent is _____. But we need two bedrooms now.
★★

B ◀)) **Listen and repeat.**

C **PAIRS Practice the conversation.**

D **PAIRS Practice the conversation again. Use different words.**

WHAT DO YOU THINK?

GROUPS What is Oscar's problem? What should he do?

STUDY Possessive nouns

Singular	Regular Plural	Irregular Plural
Peter's Restaurant **the man's** townhouse	**The employees'** schedules **The parents'** apartment	My **children's** school The **women's** restroom

Grammar Note

Use 's after singular nouns (*Oscar's parents*) and after irregular plural nouns (*the men's restroom*)

Use ' after regular plural nouns (*the students' classroom*)

PRACTICE

A **Complete the sentences. Use possessive nouns.**

1. ___Isabel and Oscar's___ children like to stay with their grandparents.
   <u>Isabel and Oscar</u>

2. His _____ apartment is far from the supermarket.
   <u>parents</u>

3. _____ appointment is at 8:00.
   <u>Oscar</u>

4. _____ parents don't live near Oscar and Isabel.
   <u>Isabel</u>

B **Complete the story about the landlady. Use possessive nouns.**

The _____landlady's_____ name is Lynn Santos. She lives
<u>1. landlady</u>

with her two children. Lynn's _____ name
<u>2. daughter</u>

is Jenny. _____ favorite thing to do is to play
<u>3. Jenny</u>

the piano. _____ son, Danny, is 15. He likes
<u>4. Lynn</u>

to go to his _____ houses and play video games.
<u>5. friends</u>

_____ father lives a few miles away. The children
<u>6. Jenny and Danny</u>

go to their _____ house every weekend.
<u>7. father</u>

WHAT ABOUT YOU?

PAIRS Tell your partner about your parents' or your friend's home.

> My parents' home is in Ethiopia. It's big . . .

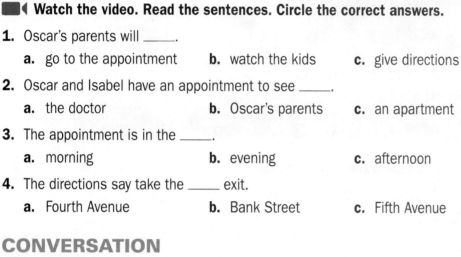

○○○○○○○ **GET READY**

Where are you now?

Think about where you live.

Is it north, south, east, or west of the building you are in now?

○○○○○○○ **WATCH**

■◀ **Watch the video. Read the sentences. Circle the correct answers.**

1. Oscar's parents will _____.

    a. go to the appointment   **b.** watch the kids   **c.** give directions

2. Oscar and Isabel have an appointment to see _____.

    a. the doctor   **b.** Oscar's parents   **c.** an apartment

3. The appointment is in the _____.

    a. morning   **b.** evening   **c.** afternoon

4. The directions say take the _____ exit.

    a. Fourth Avenue   **b.** Bank Street   **c.** Fifth Avenue

○○○○○○○ **CONVERSATION**

Ⓐ ■◀ **Watch part of the video. Complete the conversation.**

Isabel: Take Route 602 south. Get off at the Fifth Avenue exit.

Oscar: The Fifth Avenue exit?

Isabel: Yes. Then go about _____.
Turn left on Fourth Avenue. ★

Oscar: And _____? ★★

Isabel: Go straight for three lights. Then, turn right on Bank Street.

Oscar: Great. Can you print the map and the directions?

Isabel: Sure.

Ⓑ ◀))) **Listen and repeat.**

Ⓒ **PAIRS Practice the conversation.**

Ⓓ **PAIRS Practice the conversation again. Use different distances and words.**

> **Pronunciation Note**
>
> To check your understanding, you can repeat the words as a question. Make your voice go up at the end.
>
> ◀))) **Listen and repeat.**
>
> The Fifth Avenue **exit**?↗
> Turn **left**?↗

WHAT ABOUT YOU?

GROUPS Oscar's wife, Isabel, printed driving directions to the apartment. Where do you usually get directions? From a person? The Internet? A GPS device?

GET READY

When do you use a map? Give examples.

MAPS

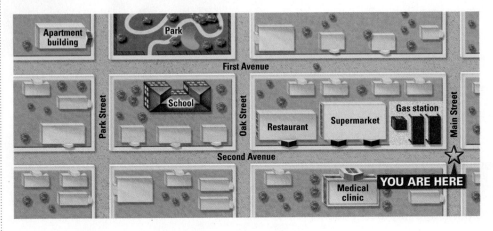

A Look at the map. Complete the conversations.

1. **A:** Where's the supermarket?

   B: It's between _____.

2. **A:** Where's the school?

   B: It's across from _____.

3. **A:** Where's the _____?

   B: Walk down Second Avenue. It's on the left.

4. **A:** Where's the _____?

   B: Walk down Second Avenue. It's on the right, next to the supermarket.

B Compare your answers with a partner.
Then practice the conversations with a partner.

C ◀)) Listen to the directions. Complete the sentences.

1. Go straight for _____ blocks.

2. Turn _____ on Park Street.

3. Go _____ block.

4. The apartment building is on your left. It's _____ the park.

WHAT DO YOU THINK?

PAIRS Imagine that you are trying to find an ATM. You ask someone for directions, but you don't understand. What should you do?

GET READY

Oscar is showing Carmen some pictures.
Guess. What kind of pictures?

WATCH

A ▄◀ **Watch the video. Was your guess correct?**

B ▄◀ **Watch the video again. Read the sentences. Circle *True* or *False*. Then correct the false sentences.**

1.	Oscar is going to look at a smaller apartment.	True	False
2.	There is a new stove in the kitchen.	True	False
3.	There are two bathtubs in the apartment.	True	False
4.	Oscar needs more space for his children.	True	False

C **Read the question about the video. Circle the answer.**

Carmen says, "Good luck tonight!" She means "_____."

a. I hope it's a nice apartment

b. I hope you find the apartment

CONVERSATION

A ▄◀ **Watch part of the video. Complete the conversation.**

Oscar: This is the kitchen, and there's a new _____.
★

Carmen: How many bathrooms are there?

Oscar: There are two bathrooms. Here's one of them.

Carmen: It's big! Is there a bathtub in the other bathroom?

Oscar: No, there isn't. But there's a shower.

Carmen: I like the apartment. There are a lot of _____.
★★

B ◀))) **Listen and repeat.**

C **PAIRS Practice the conversation.**

D **PAIRS Practice the conversation again. Use different words.**

WHAT DO YOU THINK?

PAIRS The new apartment is far from Oscar's job.
Do you think he should stay in his home or move to the new apartment? Why?

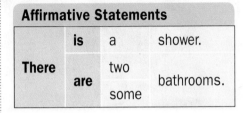

STUDY *There is / There are*

Affirmative Statements			
There	**is**	a	shower.
	are	two	bathrooms.
		some	

Negative Statements			
There	**isn't**	a	bathtub.
	aren't	any	windows.

> **Grammar Note**
>
> We can ask questions with
> ***Is there . . . ? Are there . . . ?***
> *Is there a shower?*
> *Are there any towels?*

PRACTICE

A Look at the picture. Complete the sentences below. Circle the correct answers.

1. (There are) / There aren't two people at home.
2. There is / There are many rooms.
3. There isn't / There is a TV.
4. There isn't / There aren't any pets.
5. There is / There isn't a table and chair.
6. There are / There is some stairs.

B ◀))) **Listen and check your answers. Listen and repeat.**

C Write sentences about the picture in Exercise A.
Use *there is, there isn't, there are,* or *there aren't.*

1. _There is_____ a bed.
2. _____ any windows.
3. _____ a woman on the sofa.
4. _____ any children.
5. _____ a kitchen.
6. _____ two doors.
7. _____ a man on the stairs.

WHAT ABOUT YOU?

PAIRS Tell your partner about your home. Use *there is* and *there are.*

> There is a flat-screen TV . . .

STUDY THE MODEL

A **Read Oscar's email. What is Oscar's plan for tomorrow?**

Hi, Lynn,

Thank you for showing Isabel and me the apartment on Bank Street. We really like it!

Bank Street is in a very nice neighborhood. The street is quiet. We also like the apartment. It's very sunny. We like the new kitchen, too. There is only one problem. The apartment is far from my job. Isabel and I talked. We agreed we want the apartment. We are ready to sign the lease! I will call you tomorrow.

Best,

Oscar

B **Read the Writing Tip. Read the email again. Then look at the statements. Write *MI* next to the main idea. Write *D* next to the details.**

_____ **a.** The apartment is far from his job.

_____ **b.** The apartment is in a good neighborhood.

_____ **c.** Oscar and Isabel want the apartment.

> **Writing Tip**
>
> The **main idea** is the most important idea in your writing. The **details** explain the main idea.

BEFORE YOU WRITE

Think about your house or apartment. What are your feelings about your home? Write your ideas on a sheet of paper. Then circle the most important idea.

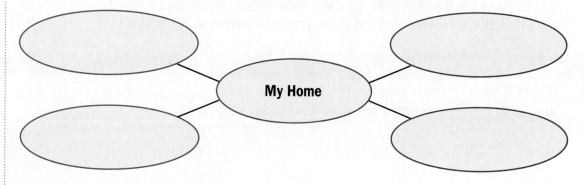

My Home

WRITE

Write about your home. Include a main idea and details. Study Oscar's email and the Writing Tip.

○○○○○○ **GET READY**

Look at the article. How many paragraphs are there?

○○○○○○ **READ**

Reading Skill

Each **paragraph** has one idea. A paragraph also includes details about the idea.

◀))) **Listen and read the article. What is a couch surfer?**

Is this couch taken?

People all over the world fall asleep on their couches. But now people around the world are sleeping on someone else's couch. It's a new way to travel. It's called couch surfing.

What is couch surfing? Couch surfing is a popular way to travel. One reason is because it's free. How does someone couch surf? They decide where they want to go. Then they talk to friends or use the Internet to find places to stay. They only stay one or two nights at each place. Then they move to a different place.

Couch surfing is very popular in the United States, Germany, France, Canada, and England. But there are couch surfers all over the world. You can also find them in North Korea, Pakistan, and even in Antarctica.

People like couch surfing because it's cheaper than staying at a hotel. But they also like it because they meet new people. And they see how people live.

○○○○○○ **AFTER YOU READ**

PAIRS **Read the Reading Skill. Find the main idea in paragraphs 2 and 3. Underline those sentences. Then share your information with the class.**

WHAT DO YOU THINK?

GROUPS What do you think about couch surfing? Are you interested in traveling this way? Why or why not?

JOB-SEEKING SKILLS
Prepare for a job interview

Sara *Today*
I have a job interview at Fresh Foods next week. I'm going to learn more about interviewing.

GET READY

Sara is reading an article about job interviews. Guess.
What are some important things to do in a job interview?

JOB INTERVIEW PREPARATIONS

A ◀))) **Listen and read the article. Did your guess match the reading?**

www.jobtips.com

Preparing for your job interview
Are you going to a job interview? Here are some tips to help you.

Before you go:
- Get a good night's sleep.
- Wear clean and neat clothes.
- Bring a copy of your job application.

Before the interview:
- Arrive 15 minutes early.
- Turn off your cell phone.
- Shake hands.
- Smile.
- Make eye contact.
- Sit up straight.
- Put your hands on the desk or in your lap.

B **Read the article again. Answer the questions.**

1. What should you do the night before the interview? _____

2. How should you dress for the interview? _____

3. What should you take to the interview? _____

4. When should you get to the interview? _____

5. What should you do when you meet the interviewer? _____

6. How should you sit? _____

PUT YOUR IDEAS TO WORK

◀))) **PAIRS** Listen to Sara practice the beginning of a job interview with a friend.
Then role play the beginning of a job interview with your partner.

GRAMMAR

In this unit, you studied:

- Possessive nouns
- *There is / there are* statements

See page 151 for your Grammar Review.

VOCABULARY See page 159 for the Unit 7 Vocabulary.

Vocabulary Learning Strategy: Make word webs

A Make word webs with the words. For example:

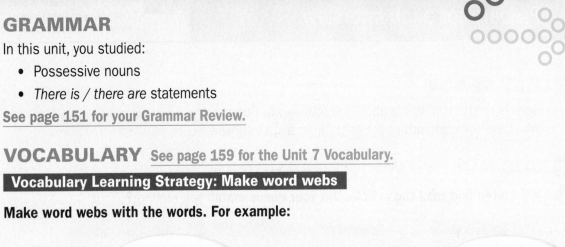

B Underline 1 word in each word map in Exercise A. Write a sentence with each word on a separate piece of paper.

My bathroom has a tub and a shower.

SPELLING See page 159 for the Unit 7 Vocabulary.

CLASS **Choose 10 words for a spelling test.**

LISTENING PLUS

A Watch each video. Write the story of Oscar's day on a separate piece of paper.

Oscar needs a new apartment. He calls a landlady.

B PAIRS **Review the conversation in Lesson 2 (see page 91).
Role play the conversation for the class.**

NOW I CAN

PAIRS See page 89 for the Unit 7 Goals. Check ☑ the things you can do.
Underline the things you want to study more. Tell your partner.

I can _____. I need more practice with _____.

8 Wen's Surprise

MY GOALS

- [ ] Call in late to work
- [ ] Talk about my abilities
- [ ] Talk about my weekend
- [ ] Identify places in the community
- [ ] Read a bus schedule
- [ ] Address an envelope
- [ ] Ask for and give prices

Go to MyEnglishLab for more practice after each lesson.

Wen Li

Wen　　　　*Today*

I'm stuck in traffic and I'm late for work. I hate to be late!

103

Call in late to work

GET READY

Wen is calling Oscar.

Guess. Why is he calling him?

WATCH

A ■◀ **Watch the video. Was your guess correct?**

B ■◀ **Watch the video again. Read the sentences. Circle *True* or *False*. Then correct the false sentences.**

1.	Wen calls Oscar and asks for a day off.	True	False
2.	There is a lot of traffic.	True	False
3.	Oscar will work for Wen.	True	False
4.	Oscar needs to talk to Wen.	True	False

CONVERSATION

A ■◀ **Watch part of the video. Complete the conversation.**

Wen: I'm sorry. I'm calling because there's a problem.

Oscar: Yes, what is it?

Wen: I'm going to be late.

I'm stuck _____.
   ★

Oscar: Your shift starts in _____ minutes.
                                    ★★

How long will it take you to get here?

Wen: I'm not sure. Maybe 25 minutes.

Oscar: OK. I'll ask Joe to stay until you get here. Thanks for calling.

Wen: Thanks, Oscar. I'm really sorry.

B ◀)) **Listen and repeat.**

C **PAIRS Practice the conversation.**

D **PAIRS Practice the conversation again. Use different places and periods of time.**

WHAT DO YOU THINK?

PAIRS Joe called in late two times this week.
What should Oscar do if Joe calls in late again?

LISTENING AND SPEAKING

Talk about your abilities

GET READY

Oscar asks Wen to come to his office.
Guess. What is Oscar going to talk about?

WATCH

A ◼◀ **Watch the video. Was your guess correct?**

B ◼◀ **Watch the video again. Read the sentences. Circle the correct answers.**

1. Oscar thanks Wen for _____.

   a. his phone call   **b.** his good work   **c.** a report

2. Oscar wants to talk to Wen about _____.

   a. being late   **b.** stocking the shelves   **c.** a promotion

3. Oscar wants to make Wen a _____ produce associate.

   a. senior   **b.** junior   **c.** part-time

4. Wen will have training to learn about his new _____.

   a. schedule   **b.** job   **c.** manager

CONVERSATION

A ◼◀ **Watch part of the video. Complete the conversation.**

Oscar: You're an excellent produce associate.

Wen: Thank you.

Oscar: You can _____.

                   ★

        You can stock any part of the produce department.

Wen: I really like my job.

Oscar: And you have good communication skills.

Wen: Thanks. I enjoy _____.
                            ★★

Oscar: I want to give you a promotion.

B ◀)) **Listen and repeat.**

C **PAIRS Practice the conversation.**

D **PAIRS Practice the conversation again. Use different words.**

Pronunciation Note
Can usually has a short, quiet vowel sound:
"I c'n help"
Can't always has a long, clear vowel sound:
"I **can't** help."
◀)) **Listen and repeat.**
You can take inventory.
You can stock produce.

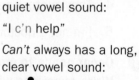

WHAT DO YOU THINK?

GROUPS Wen gets a promotion. What are some reasons people get promotions?
Make a list.

GRAMMAR

③ Can / Can't

 STUDY *Can / Can't*

Affirmative Statements

I He Wen We You They	**can**	**help**	customers.

Negative Statements

I He Wen We You They	**can't**	**fill out**	reports.

Grammar Note

Can shows ability.
can't = cannot

Yes / No Questions

Can	you she they	**operate**	a forklift?

Short Answers

Yes,	I we she they	**can.**	**No,**	I we she they	**can't.**

PRACTICE

A Complete the sentences. Use *can* or *can't.*

1. She's a cashier. She ____can____ use a cash register.

2. He's a student. He _____ speak a little English.

3. We're pharmacists. We _____ fill prescriptions.

4. They're stocking associates. They _____ operate a forklift.

5. I'm not a doctor. I _____ help patients.

B Oscar needs to make a list of job interview questions.
Write questions with *Can.*

1. operate a forklift   _Can you operate a forklift?_____

2. stock produce   _____

3. help customers   _____

4. take inventory   _____

C **PAIRS** Take turns. Ask and answer the questions in Exercise B. Use short answers.

WHAT ABOUT YOU?

GROUPS Choose a job. Make a list of interview questions for that job.
Then find a different classmate. Take turns asking your questions.

LISTENING AND SPEAKING

Talk about your weekend

GET READY

Carmen and Wen are talking about their weekends.

What do you do on weekends?

WATCH

■◄ **Watch the video. Read the sentences. Circle *True* or *False*. Then correct the false sentences.**

1.	Carmen had a busy weekend.	True	False
2.	Wen went to the library.	True	False
3.	Wen had dinner with his friends.	True	False
4.	Carmen and her daughters went shopping.	True	False
5.	Carmen did homework on Sunday.	True	False
6.	Wen stayed home on Sunday.	True	False

CONVERSATION

A ■◄ **Watch part of the video. Complete the conversation.**

Carmen: How was your weekend?

Wen: Great.

Carmen: What did you do?

Wen: On Saturday, I was at the gym. Then I went to a

_____ with some friends.
★
How about you?

Carmen: On Saturday, I cleaned the house. Then my daughters

and I went to a _____.
★★
Later we made dinner for my parents.

B ◄))) **Listen and repeat.**

C **PAIRS** **Practice the conversation.**

D **PAIRS** **Practice the conversation again. Use different places and activities.**

WHAT ABOUT YOU?

GROUPS Carmen likes to be busy on weekends. What about you? Are you busy or do you stay home and relax?

Be, have, go: Simple past

○○○○○ **STUDY** *Be, have, go:* Simple past

Be: Simple past

Affirmative Statements		
I He She It	**was**	
		busy.
We You They	**were**	

Negative Statements		
I He She It	**wasn't**	
		busy.
We You They	**weren't**	

Grammar Note
Irregular verbs *is* ⟶ *was* *have* ⟶ *had* *go* ⟶ *went*

Have, go: Simple past

Affirmative Statements		
I	**had**	lunch downtown.
She	**went**	to the movies.

Negative Statements			
I	**didn't**	**have**	lunch downtown.
She		**go**	to the movies.

○○○○○ **PRACTICE**

A **Circle the correct words.**

1. They was / (were) very tired on Sunday night.

2. He wasn't / weren't busy last weekend.

3. I wasn't / weren't late for work yesterday.

4. We was / were sick last week.

5. You was / were early today.

6. It wasn't / weren't hot yesterday.

B **Complete the sentences. Use the simple past of *be, have,* or *go.***

Joe and his friends ____had____ a fun weekend. On Saturday, they _____ to
                      1.   2.

the shopping mall. They _____ very hungry, so they _____ to any
                         3.   4.

restaurants. They ate at home later. Joe _____ to a lot of stores, but he
                                           5.

_____ money, so he didn't buy anything. On Sunday, the weather _____
  6.   7.

warm and sunny. Joe and his friends _____ to the park and played soccer.
                                       8.

WHAT ABOUT YOU?

PAIRS Take turns. Talk about last weekend. Use *be, have, go* and regular verbs.

Identify places in the community

GET READY

Does your neighborhood or community have a name? What is it?

PLACES IN THE COMMUNITY

A Look at the places in the community. What do you do in each place?
Write the letter.

a. a post office

b. a gas station

c. a laundromat

d. a hospital

e. a library

f. a police station

g. a fire station

h. a bank

_____ **1.** You wash clothes.

_____ **2.** You borrow books and magazines.

_____ **3.** You get gas for your car.

_____ **4.** You get help with a crime.

_____ **5.** You keep money.

_____ **6.** You get help for a fire.

_____ **7.** You get help with a medical emergency.

_____ **8.** You mail a letter or package.

B ◀)) **Listen. Complete the conversations.**

Conversation 1

A: Excuse me. Where's the _____?

B: It's on Duke Street. Next to the laundromat.

A: Thanks.

Conversation 2

A: Hello. Is there a _____ near here?

B: Yes. On the corner of 28th Street and Lee Highway.

A: Thank you.

> **Speaking Note**
>
> Ask someone to speak
> more slowly by saying:
> *Could you speak more
> slowly, please?*

C **PAIRS Practice the conversations. Then make new conversations
with the places in Exercise A.**

WHAT ABOUT YOU?

PAIRS Take turns. Say where the places in Exercise A are in your community.

Read a bus schedule

GET READY

Do you take the bus? Where do you go?

BUS SCHEDULES

A   Read the schedules. Answer the questions.

B26 and B27x Weekday Service Westbound

Bus	Seven Corners Hospital	Washington Ave. & Broad St.	Broad St. Post Office	Hay Ave. & Broad St.	West Falls Metro Station
B26	5:30	5:45	5:55	5:58	6:05
B27 Express	5:40	—	—	—	6:00

B28 Weekday Service Westbound

Bus	First Street	Second Street	Oak Street	West Street Police Station	Fifth Street Bus Station
B28	5:30	—	5:55	6:02	6:10

1. How many buses are on the schedules? _____
2. What direction are the buses going? _____
3. What time does the B26 leave Seven Corners Hospital? _____
4. How many stops does the B27 Express make? _____
5. How long does the express bus take to go from the hospital to the metro station? _____
6. How many stops does the B28 make? _____
7. How long does the B28 take from First Street to the bus station? _____

B   **PAIRS Write 5 more questions about the information in the bus schedule. Then ask a partner your questions.**

WHAT ABOUT YOU?

GROUPS What types of transportation are available where you live? Which do you use?

> There are buses and subways. I use . . .

PRACTICAL SKILLS

Address an envelope

8

GET READY

Where is the post office in your community?

ENVELOPES

Mr. David Smith
3592 28th St.
Alexandria, VA 22302

Mrs. Barbara Anderson
2930 Rose Avenue
Apartment 3
Los Angeles, CA 90243

A **Read the envelope. Answer the questions.**

1. Who is sending the letter? _____

2. Who is the letter for? _____

3. What is David Smith's street address? _____

4. What is Barbara Anderson's title? _____

B **You are writing to a friend or family member. Address the envelope to that person. Write your return address.**

> **Speaking Note**
>
> Ask for clarification by asking for spelling. *Could you spell that, please?*

_____

_____

_____

_____

_____

_____

_____

WHAT DO YOU THINK?

PAIRS Imagine you receive a letter at your house, but it is not for you or anyone who lives with you. What should you do?

LISTENING AND SPEAKING

Ask for and give prices

GET READY

Wen is helping a customer.

Guess. Why is the customer upset?

WATCH

A ◼◀ **Watch the video. Was your guess correct?**

B ◼◀ **Watch the video again. Read the sentences. Circle the correct answers.**

1. The cucumbers are _____.
   - **a.** on special
   - **b.** regular price
   - **c.** expensive

2. The tomatoes are _____.
   - **a.** 69¢ a pound
   - **b.** $1.89 a pound
   - **c.** 79¢ a pound

3. The avocados are _____.
   - **a.** $1.25 each
   - **b.** $1.25 a pound
   - **c.** $1.25 for two

4. The customer thinks the prices are _____.
   - **a.** great
   - **b.** low
   - **c.** high

CONVERSATION

A ◼◀ **Watch part of the video. Complete the conversation.**

Customer: Excuse me. How much are the cucumbers?

Wen: They're three for a dollar.

Customer: Three for a dollar?

Wen: Yes. They're on special this week.

Customer: How much is the _____?
　　　　　　　　　　　　　　　　★

Wen: _____.
　　　　　★★

> **Pronunciation Note**
>
> Notice the different vowel sounds in *much* and *dollars*.
>
> ◀)) **Listen and repeat.**
>
> | much | other | customer |
> |------|-------|----------|
> | dollar | not | avocado |

B ◀)) **Listen and repeat.**

C **PAIRS** Practice the conversation.

D **PAIRS** Practice the conversation again. Use different vegetables and prices.

WHAT DO YOU THINK?

GROUPS Imagine you and your classmates are store managers.

What are different ways to help a customer who is upset? Make a list.

GET READY

What is important to you when you go to a restaurant?
What restaurants do you like or dislike? Why?

READ

◀)) **Listen and read the article. How many people wrote a restaurant review?**

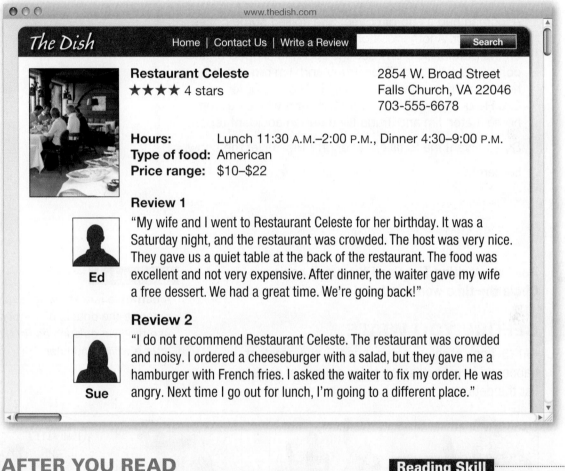

www.thedish.com

The Dish   Home | Contact Us | Write a Review   Search

Restaurant Celeste   2854 W. Broad Street
★★★★ 4 stars   Falls Church, VA 22046
          703-555-6678

Hours: Lunch 11:30 A.M.–2:00 P.M., Dinner 4:30–9:00 P.M.
Type of food: American
Price range: $10–$22

Review 1
Ed
"My wife and I went to Restaurant Celeste for her birthday. It was a Saturday night, and the restaurant was crowded. The host was very nice. They gave us a quiet table at the back of the restaurant. The food was excellent and not very expensive. After dinner, the waiter gave my wife a free dessert. We had a great time. We're going back!"

Review 2
Sue
"I do not recommend Restaurant Celeste. The restaurant was crowded and noisy. I ordered a cheeseburger with a salad, but they gave me a hamburger with French fries. I asked the waiter to fix my order. He was angry. Next time I go out for lunch, I'm going to a different place."

AFTER YOU READ

PAIRS Read the Reading Skill. Read each restaurant review again. Underline the words that support each writer's point of view.

Reading Skill

A writer has a **point of view**. Look for words that show the writer's opinion or belief.

WHAT DO YOU THINK?

GROUPS Think about a restaurant you went to. How was the food?
Share your point of view with your classmates.

Write a narrative

STUDY THE MODEL

A **Read Joe's email. Did someone call 911?**

Dear Oscar:

I saw the accident in the Deli Department today. Here are the details.

A woman had a cup of coffee. She spilled some coffee on the floor. Another customer was next to her. He was on the phone. He didn't see the spill and slipped on the coffee. He fell down. Then Truda and Jim ran over to help him. They wanted to call 911. The customer was OK. He did not want to call 911. After a while, he went home. Later Jim and Truda filled out an accident report.

Do you want me to fill out a report? Please let me know.

Sincerely,

Joe

B **Read the Writing Tip. Read the email again. Circle the time words in Joe's email.**

BEFORE YOU WRITE

PAIRS Look at the pictures. Imagine the accident happened in your classroom. On a piece of paper, list the details.

> **Writing Tip**
>
> A **narrative** is a story. To help organize the details of a story, use time words such as *first*, *then*, *after a while*, and *later*.

WRITE

Write a narrative. Tell the story of the accident. Use your list of details and time words. Study Joe's email and the Writing Tip.

Sara *Today*
I have a job interview at 4:00 today. I'm a little nervous!

GET READY

Sara is at a job interview. Some people get nervous at job interviews. What are some things you can do to help you relax?

JOB INTERVIEW: PART 1

A ◀)) **Listen and read part of the interview.**
What kind of job does Sara want?

Manager: So, you're applying for the customer service representative job. I see that you have experience in a supermarket.

Sara: Yes. I worked at the Venice Market for four years from May 2006 to July 2010. I was a cashier.

Manager: OK. Tell me about your skills. Can you use a cash register and a computer?

Sara: Yes, I can. And I have good people skills.

Manager: Can you give me an example?

Sara: Yes. Sometimes customers are not polite. But I'm always very polite with customers.

Manager: Tell me about your education.

Sara: I graduated from high school.

Manager: Are you going to school now?

Sara: Yes. I'm taking computer classes at night.

B ◀)) **Listen and read again. Circle *True* or *False*.**
Then correct the false sentences.

1. Sara can use a cash register and a computer.	True	False
2. She is sometimes polite with customers.	True	False
3. Sara is taking classes at night.	True	False
4. She worked in a supermarket from 2006 to 2010.	True	False

PUT YOUR IDEAS TO WORK

PAIRS Take turns. Choose a job you want. Interview your partner.
Use the conversation in Exercise A.

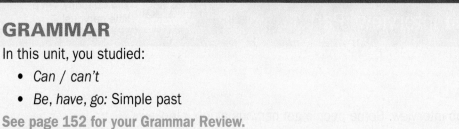

GRAMMAR

In this unit, you studied:

- *Can / can't*
- *Be, have, go:* Simple past

See page 152 for your Grammar Review.

VOCABULARY See page 159 for the Unit 8 Vocabulary.

Vocabulary Learning Strategy: Draw pictures

A Choose 10 words from the list. In your notebook, draw pictures of them. Write the words next to them.

B Underline 5 words from Exercise A. Write a sentence with each word on a separate piece of paper.

SPELLING See page 159 for the Unit 8 Vocabulary.

CLASS Choose 10 words for a spelling test.

LISTENING PLUS

A Watch each video. Write the story of Wen's day on a separate piece of paper.

Wen is stuck in traffic. He calls Oscar.

B **PAIRS** Review the conversations in Lesson 6 (see page 109). Role play the conversation for the class.

NOW I CAN

PAIRS See page 103 for the Unit 8 Goals. Check ☑ the things you can do. Underline the things you want to study more. Tell your partner.

> I can _____. I need more practice with _____.

9 Truda Asks for Help

MY GOALS

- ☐ Talk about good and bad news
- ☐ Report a housing problem
- ☐ Talk about forms at work
- ☐ Read a pay stub
- ☐ Complete an emergency contact form
- ☐ Call 911 to report an emergency
- ☐ Read warning signs

Go to MyEnglishLab for more practice after each lesson.

Truda Mazur

Truda   *Today*
What a crazy day! I can't believe everything that's happening.

1

Talk about good and bad news

GET READY

Truda's husband calls her at work.
Guess. Why is he calling?

WATCH

A ◼◀ **Watch the video. Was your guess correct?**

B ◼◀ **Watch the video again. Read the sentences. Circle *True* or *False*. Then correct the false sentences.**

1.	Truda's husband has good and bad news.	True	False
2.	Truda's husband is working at the Tower Hotel right now.	True	False
3.	Truda's husband had a car accident.	True	False
4.	Truda will call the landlord during her lunch break.	True	False

CONVERSATION

A ◼◀ **Watch part of the video. Complete the conversation.**

Stefan: I have _____ news. Guess what happened.
                              ★

Truda: What?

Stefan: I got the custodian job at the Tower Hotel.
I start on Friday.

Truda: Fantastic! That's great news!
We have to celebrate this weekend!

Stefan: OK. But I also have some bad news.
My friend Peter was in an accident.

Truda: _____!
                      ★★

B ◀)) **Listen and repeat.**

C **PAIRS Practice the conversation.**

D **PAIRS Practice the conversation again. Use different words to talk about good and bad news.**

Pronunciation Note

To show strong feeling, the voice goes up very high and then goes down.

◀)) **Listen and repeat.**

Fantastic!

Great!

Oh, no!

WHAT DO YOU THINK?

GROUPS Truda's husband, Stefan, can't take care of their children in the afternoon because he has a new job. What can Truda and Stefan do?

Report a housing problem

GET READY

Truda calls her landlord about some problems in her apartment.

Guess. What are the problems?

WATCH

A ◼◀ Watch the video. Was your guess correct?

B ◼◀ Watch the video again. Read the sentences. Circle the correct answers.

1. The lock on the _____ door isn't working.

   a. front   **b.** bathroom   **c.** bedroom

2. The _____ is leaking.

   a. shower   **b.** faucet   **c.** toilet

3. The _____ is cracked.

   a. window   **b.** door   **c.** closet

4. The landlord will send someone over _____.

   a. this morning   **b.** this afternoon   **c.** tomorrow

> ### Pronunciation Note
>
> Notice how we link *is* or *are* to the word before it.
>
> ◀))) **Listen and repeat.**
>
> This is Tom.
>
> There are some problems.
>
> The faucet is leaking.

CONVERSATION

A ◼◀ Watch part of the video. Complete the conversation.

Truda: I'm calling because there are some problems in our apartment.

Landlord: Oh?

Truda: The lock on the front door is broken. We have to push it really hard.

     And the _____ is leaking.
               ★

Landlord: Are there any other problems?

Truda: The bathroom window is _____.
                               ★★

B ◀))) **Listen and repeat.**

C PAIRS Practice the conversation.

D PAIRS Practice the conversation again. Use different words.

WHAT DO YOU THINK?

GROUPS Who fixes the problems in your home?

> I fix . . .   My wife fixes . . .

GRAMMAR

3 Present continuous: Statements

STUDY Present continuous: Statements

Subject	Be	(Not)	Verb + -ing		Contractions		
I	am				I'm		
He	is				He's		
We They You	are	(not)	**working**	right now.	We're They're You're	(not)	**working** right now.
The faucet It	is		**leaking**		It's		**leaking**

Grammar Note

More contractions

*The lock **isn't** working.*   *They **aren't** working.*

PRACTICE

A **Complete the sentences about the supermarket. Use the present continuous.**

1. The customer ___*is ordering*___ a sandwich.
   _{order}

2. The clerks _____ the shelves. They _____ a break.
   _{not / stock}   _{take}

3. We _____ in a long line. We're in a short line.
   _{not / wait}

4. I _____ for my items with my ATM card.
   _{pay}

5. You _____ vegetables, but you _____ fruit.
   _{not / buy}   _{buy}

B **What are Truda's neighbors doing? Write sentences with the present continuous. Use contractions.**

1. Ms. Rubio is in Apt. 2A.   ___*She's reading the newspaper.*___
   _{read the newspaper}

2. Mr. and Mrs. Silver are in Apt. 2C.   _____
   _{eat lunch}

3. Charlie is in Apt. 2D.   _____
   _{check email}

4. Mrs. Gomez is in Apt. 1E.   Her sink _____
   _{leak}

WHAT ABOUT YOU?

PAIRS Think about your neighborhood. What is happening now?

People are going
to work . . .

LISTENING AND SPEAKING

Talk about forms at work

GET READY

Employees need to fill out forms when they start a new job.
What kinds of forms do they fill out?

WATCH

⬛◀ **Watch the video. Read the sentences. Circle *True* or *False*. Then correct the false sentences.**

1.	Jim asks Truda to fill out a pay stub.	True	False
2.	Truda should give three names as contacts.	True	False
3.	Truda gets paid every Thursday.	True	False
4.	Truda should look at her pay stub carefully.	True	False
5.	Jim will look at Truda's pay stub, too.	True	False

CONVERSATION

A ⬛◀ **Watch part of the video. Complete the conversation.**

Jim: Do you have a minute? I need you to fill out some forms.

Truda: An emergency contact form . . . OK.

Jim: You need to give two contact names and information.

And there is some information about _____ to read, also.
＊

Truda: OK. Thanks.

Jim: I'll need all of the forms by _____.
＊＊

Truda: OK.

B ◀)) **Listen and repeat.**

C **PAIRS** **Practice the conversation.**

D **PAIRS** **Practice the conversation again. Use different information and pay periods.**

WHAT DO YOU THINK?

PAIRS Truda gets her first paycheck. She thinks there is a mistake. What should she do?

> I think she should . . .

5 Read a pay stub

Think about your job or a friend's job. Do you get paid by check? With cash?

PAYCHECKS

A Read the pay stub. What is Truda's total pay for this pay period?

Fresh Foods Supermarket	Pay Date: 2/28/2015
7460 Duke Street	
Alexandria, VA 22304	

Employee: Truda Mazur	Pay Period Start: 2/13/2015
Employee SSN: 000-72-3056	Pay Period End: 2/27/2015

	Hours	Pay Rate	Deductions	Total
Regular Hours	80	$13.25		1,060.00
Overtime Hours	1	$16.75		16.75
Total Pay				1,076.75
Federal Taxes			129.21	
FICA			86.14	
State Income Tax			39.16	
Medical Insurance			43.51	
Total Deductions			298.02	
NET PAY				778.73

B Read the pay stub again. Circle *True* or *False*. Then correct the false statements.

1. Truda makes $15.00 an hour.　　　　　　　　　　　　True　　False

2. This pay period includes February 14.　　　　　　　True　　False

3. Truda worked three hours of overtime this pay period.　True　　False

4. Federal taxes and state income tax are deductions.　　True　　False

5. For this pay period Truda took home $778.73　　　　True　　False

Speaking Note

It's important to make sure information is correct. If you think there is a mistake, you can say:

I'm not sure this is correct.
I think there is a mistake.
This information is incorrect.

WHAT DO YOU THINK?

GROUPS Truda earned $1,076.75 this pay period. Look at the tax deductions. Give examples of what taxes are used for in your community and in your state.

6

Complete an emergency contact form

GET READY

Think about family and friends who live near you.
Who can be a contact person in case you have an emergency?

EMERGENCY CONTACT FORMS

A Read the form. Answer the questions.

Fresh Foods Supermarket
Emergency Contact Form

Employee: Truda Mazur   **Date:** 03/06/2015

Contact Information

Name	Relationship	Day phone	Evening phone	Cell
Stefan Mazur	husband	703-555-1103	703-555-9378	703-555-3144
Ana Barlik	sister	202-555-3410	202-555-8264	no

1. Who is this form for? _____

2. Who is Stefan Mazur? _____

3. Who is Ana Barlik? _____

4. If there is an emergency at 2:00 P.M., which numbers should Truda's boss, Jim, call?

   _____ _____

5. If there is an emergency at 7:00 P.M., which numbers should Jim call?

   _____ _____

B Fill in the form with your information. Use real or made up information.

Emergency Contact Form

Employee: **Date:**

Contact Information

Name	Relationship	Day phone	Evening phone	Cell

WHAT ABOUT YOU?

PAIRS Where do you have your emergency contact information? In your wallet?
In your purse? Where do people in your family have their information?

LISTENING AND SPEAKING

Call 911 to report an emergency

GET READY

There is an emergency.
Guess. What is happening?

WATCH

A ◼◀ **Watch the video.
Was your guess correct?**

B ◼◀ **Watch the video again. Put the sentences in order.
Write 1, 2, 3, or 4.**

_____ Truda calls 911.

_____ Jim is unconscious.

_____ The emergency operator sends an ambulance.

_____ Truda asks Wen to help.

CONVERSATION

A ◼◀ **Watch part of the video. Complete the conversation.**

Operator: 911. What's the address of your emergency?

Truda: I'm at the Fresh Foods supermarket.
The address is 7460 Duke Street.

Operator: What's _____★_____?

Truda: My coworker is _____★★_____.

Operator: Where is your coworker now?

Truda: He's next to me. My other coworker is with him.

B ◀))) **Listen and repeat.**

C PAIRS **Practice the conversation. Use your own address.**

D PAIRS **Practice the conversation again. Use new words and emergencies.**

WHAT DO YOU THINK?

GROUPS Imagine. You call 911 to report an emergency.
You don't understand the operator's questions. What can you do?

You can . . .

STUDY Object pronouns

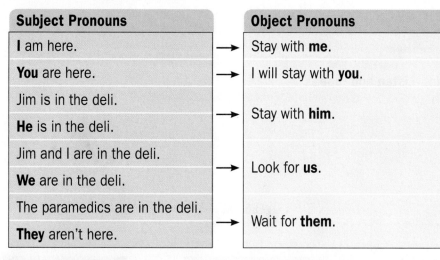

Subject Pronouns	Object Pronouns
I am here.	→ Stay with **me**.
You are here.	→ I will stay with **you**.
Jim is in the deli.	
He is in the deli.	→ Stay with **him**.
Jim and I are in the deli.	
We are in the deli.	→ Look for **us**.
The paramedics are in the deli.	
They aren't here.	→ Wait for **them**.

Grammar Note

I, you, he, she, it, we, and *they* are subject pronouns.
Me, you, him, her, it, us, and *them* are object pronouns.

PRACTICE

A **Circle the correct pronouns.**

1. Me /(I) work at Fresh Foods. Everyone is nice.

2. Saba is my good friend. I like to eat lunch with she / her.

3. We / Us are produce associates.

4. He / Him and I are coworkers. We both live nearby.

5. Please help they / them. They need to move boxes.

B ◀))) **Listen and check your answers.**

C **Complete the sentences. Write *me*, *her*, *him*, *us*, or *them*.**

1. She is hurt. Stay with _____ *her* _____.

2. They had an accident. Don't move _____.

3. We need help! Please help _____!

4. His head is bleeding. Don't lift _____.

5. I'm in the store. Please look for _____ in the Deli Department.

D ◀))) **Listen and check your answers.**

WHAT ABOUT YOU?

GROUPS Have you or anyone you known called 911? What was the emergency?

GET READY

What kinds of warning signs do you see at your work or at your school?

WARNING SIGNS

A ◀)) **Listen and point. Listen and repeat.**

1.

2.

3.

4.

5.

6.

B ◀)) **Listen. Circle the letter of the correct sign.**

1. **a.** Authorized personnel only

   b. No trespassing

2. **a.** Employees must wear gloves

   b. Employees must wash hands

3. **a.** Authorized personnel only

   b. Fire door, keep closed

C **PAIRS Say where you can see each sign.**

> Sign 1 is in a deli department.

Speaking Note

To confirm that you understand, use an expression such as:

OK, Got it, or *I understand.*

WHAT ABOUT YOU?

GROUPS Think about warning signs in your country.
Are they the same as or different from the signs in the U.S.?

Express thanks

STUDY THE MODEL

A **Read the email. Why is Jim writing this email?**

From: Jim Robbins
Date: July 14, 2015 2:20 P.M.
Subj: Thank you

Dear Friends,

Thank you so much for thinking about me. I really appreciate the cards and the balloons. They make me feel better.

I was in the hospital for two days. The doctors did many tests. I have some problems with my heart. I am taking medication now. Tomorrow I have a follow-up doctor's appointment.

I'm home now, and I feel much better. I'm resting a lot. I miss Fresh Foods and my friends and coworkers. You are all great people! I hope that I can come back to work next week.

Thank you so much for your kindness.

Jim

B **Read the Writing Tip. Read the email again. What is Jim thanking his coworkers for? Underline details and words and phrases that show thanks.**

Writing Tip

Give details in a **thank you letter** to say why you are writing. Use words such as *thank you* and *I appreciate*.

BEFORE YOU WRITE

PAIRS Think of someone you want to thank. It can be a parent, a relative, a friend, or a coworker. Tell your partner why you are saying thank you to this person. Give details.

WRITE

Write a thank you letter. Use words such as *thank you* and *I appreciate*, and give details. Study Jim's thank you note and the Writing Tip.

READING

11 Identify author's purpose

GET READY

Truda called 911 about an emergency at work.
What are some examples of emergencies?

READ

🔊 **Listen and read the article. Look at the cartoon. Why is it funny?**

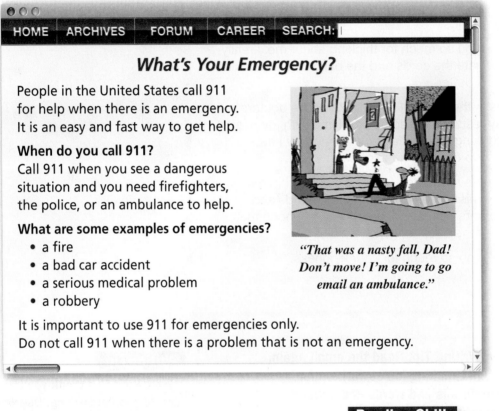

| HOME | ARCHIVES | FORUM | CAREER | SEARCH: | |

What's Your Emergency?

People in the United States call 911
for help when there is an emergency.
It is an easy and fast way to get help.

When do you call 911?
Call 911 when you see a dangerous
situation and you need firefighters,
the police, or an ambulance to help.

What are some examples of emergencies?
- a fire
- a bad car accident
- a serious medical problem
- a robbery

*"That was a nasty fall, Dad!
Don't move! I'm going to go
email an ambulance."*

It is important to use 911 for emergencies only.
Do not call 911 when there is a problem that is not an emergency.

AFTER YOU READ

**Read the Reading Skill. Then read the article again.
What is the main purpose this article?
Circle the correct answer.**

a. to give advice   **b.** to tell a story   **c.** to give information

> **Reading Skill**
>
> A text always has a **purpose**. It can be to give information, to tell a story, to give advice, or to tell a joke.

WHAT DO YOU THINK?

GROUPS Look at each problem. Should you call 911?
What should you do if it is not an emergency?

(a robbery   a flat tire   a broken finger   a fire)

Sara *Today*
I'm glad I prepared for my job interview. I think I'm doing well!

GET READY

Think about job interviews. What questions do interviewers ask?

JOB INTERVIEW: PART 2

A ◀))) **Listen and read the last part of the interview. When can Sara start?**

Manager: Do you want to work part-time or full-time?

Sara: Part-time.

Manager: Which shift can you work: morning? afternoon? night?

Sara: The morning shift is good for me.

Manager: And when can you start working?

Sara: I can start immediately.

Manager: Some final questions. Are you 18 years old or older?

Sara: Yes, I am.

Manager: And are you legally able to work in the United States?

Sara: Yes, I am.

Manager: Have you ever served in the U.S. military?

Sara: No. I haven't.

B ◀))) **Listen and read again. Circle the correct answers.**

1. Sara wants to work _____.
   a. part-time   b. full-time

2. Sara wants the _____ shift.
   a. morning   b. afternoon   c. evening

3. Sara is _____ than 18 years old.
   a. younger   b. older

4. Sara _____ legally work in the U.S.
   a. can not   b. can

5. Sara _____ served in the United States military.
   a. has   b. never

PUT YOUR IDEAS TO WORK

PAIRS Take turns. Choose a job you want. Interview your partner. Use the conversation in Exercise A.

UNIT 9 REVIEW

GRAMMAR

In this unit, you studied:

- Present continuous: Statements
- Object pronouns

See page 153 for your Grammar Review.

VOCABULARY See page 160 for the Unit 9 Vocabulary.

Vocabulary Learning Strategy: Group by context

A **Choose words from the list and put them into these groups:**

Words on pay stubs: _Deductions_____

Words on signs: _Caution_____

Words in the newspaper: _Robbery_____

Words in conversations: _Fantastic_____

Words on a maintenance form: _Leak_____

B **Underline 5 words from Exercise A. Write a sentence with each word on a separate piece of paper.**

SPELLING See page 160 for the Unit 9 Vocabulary.

CLASS Choose 10 words for a spelling test.

LISTENING PLUS

A **Watch each video. Write the story of Truda's day on a separate piece of paper.**

> _Truda's husband calls her at work. He has good news._

B **PAIRS** Review the conversation in Lesson 1 (see page 118).
Role play the conversation for the class.

NOW I CAN

PAIRS See page 117 for the Unit 9 Goals. Check ☑ the things you can do.
Underline the things you want to study more. Tell your partner.

> I can _____. I need more practice with _____.

10 Carmen Gets an Invitation

MY GOALS

- ☐ Talk about clothing
- ☐ Read clothing sizes
- ☐ Return something to the store
- ☐ Say why I am returning something
- ☐ Read a menu
- ☐ Order from a menu
- ☐ Accept an invitation

Go to MyEnglishLab for more practice after each lesson.

 Carmen Vasquez

Carmen *Today*
I can't wait for Oscar's party. We have many things to celebrate!

GET READY

Carmen is going shopping with her daughters.
Guess. What are they going to buy?

WATCH

A ◼◀ Watch the video. Was your guess correct?

B ◼◀ Watch the video again. Read the sentences. Circle *True* or *False*.
Then correct the false sentences.

1.	Carmen's daughters need new clothes.	True	False
2.	Carmen will take the girls shopping after lunch.	True	False
3.	The girls need socks.	True	False
4.	Carmen will pick up her mother at 10:30.	True	False

CONVERSATION

A ◼◀ Watch part of the video again. Complete the conversation.

Mom: What do the girls need?

Carmen: I think they both need _____.
★

Mom: They're growing so fast! Do they need anything else?

Carmen: Well, Salma wants some new shorts and a belt.
And Lisa wants new jeans.

Mom: Do they need _____?
★★

Carmen: No, they don't.

B ◀)) Listen and repeat.

C PAIRS Practice the conversation.

D PAIRS Practice the conversation again. Use different clothing items.

WHAT DO YOU THINK?

GROUPS Carmen's daughter Lisa wants expensive jeans. She says all the girls
have these jeans. Carmen wants to be careful of how much money they spend.
What should she do?

She should . . .

Simple present: *Wh-* questions

STUDY Simple present: *Wh-* questions

Wh- questions

What	do	I we you they	need?
	does	he she	

Where	does	she	shop?
When	do	the stores they	open?

> **Grammar Note**
>
> We answer *Wh-* questions with long answers or short answers.
> ***What does Salma need?***
> *Shorts and a belt.*   *She needs shorts and a belt.*

PRACTICE

A Complete the questions. Write *do* or *does*.

1. What ____do____ you want?

2. Where _____ they live?

3. When _____ she work?

4. Where _____ he go to school?

5. What _____ we need to buy?

6. When _____ you eat lunch?

B Complete the conversations. Write the questions.

1. **A:** Where _does she work?_____

   B: She works in the dairy department.

2. **A:** When _____?

   B: I work from 7:00 to 3:00.

3. **A:** What _____?

   B: The customer needs a price check.

4. **A:** Where _____?

   B: They live in Alexandria.

5. **A:** When _____?

   B: She takes a break at 10:30.

6. **A:** What _____?

   B: He wants a blue sweater.

C ◀)) **Listen and check your answers. Then practice the conversations with a partner.**

WHAT ABOUT YOU?

PAIRS Ask your partner about shopping. Use *When, Where,* and *What.*

When do you go shopping?   What do you buy?

3

Read clothing sizes

GET READY

How often do you shop for clothing? What do you buy most often?

CLOTHING SIZES

A ◀)) **Listen and point. Listen and repeat.**

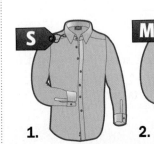

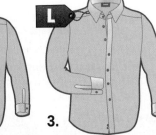

1.   2.   3.   4.

B ◀)) **Listen and complete the conversations.**

Conversation 1

Customer: Excuse me. Can you help me?

Salesperson: Yes.

Customer: Do you have this _____ in a _____?

Salesperson: Yes, we do.

Conversation 2

Salesperson: Hello. Can I help you?

Customer: Yes. I'm looking for a size _____.

Salesperson: I'm sorry. There aren't any left in that size.

> **Speaking Note**
>
> To ask someone to repeat information say:
> *What's the size again, please?*

C **PAIRS Practice the conversations. Use new clothing items.**

WHAT ABOUT YOU?

GROUPS Think about shopping in your country.
Are the sizes used for clothing the same or different?

> The sizes in my country are
> different. We use . . .

LISTENING AND SPEAKING

4 Return something to the store

GET READY

Carmen is talking to Saba at the Customer Service Desk.

Guess. What does Carmen want?

WATCH

A ▶ **Watch the video. Was your guess correct?**

B ▶ **Watch the video again. Complete the sentences with words from the box.**

> receipt   credit   card   return   exchange

1. Carmen wants to _____ an item.

2. Carmen does not want to _____ the item.

3. Carmen doesn't have the _____.

4. Saba gives Carmen store _____.

5. Saba hands Carmen a gift _____.

CONVERSATION

A ▶ **Watch part of the video again. Complete the conversation.**

Saba: Hi, Carmen. Can I help you?

Carmen: Hi, Saba. I need to return these _____.
⭐

Saba: Do you want to exchange them? Or do you need anything else?

Carmen: No, thanks. I'd like a refund. But I don't have my receipt.

Saba: _____. I can give you store credit.
⭐⭐

Carmen: Great.

B ◀)) **Listen and repeat.**

C **PAIRS** Practice the conversation. Use your own names.

D **PAIRS** Practice the conversation again. Use different items and words.

WHAT DO YOU THINK?

GROUPS Talk about returning items in your country.
What can and can't you return?
Do you always need a receipt?

> In my country, you can return . . .

Say why you are returning something

GET READY

Do you ever return clothes to a store? Why?

RETURN ITEMS TO A STORE

A ◀))) **Listen and point. Listen and repeat.**

B ◀))) **Listen and complete the conversation.**

Customer: I'd like to return this _____.

Salesperson: Sure. What's the problem?

Customer: _____

Salesperson: Do you want to look for anything else?

Customer: No, thank you.

Salesperson: Do you have your receipt?

Customer: Yes. Here it is.

> **Speaking Note**
>
> To confirm that you understand, repeat what you heard.
>
> *So, this sweater is too big?*

C **PAIRS** Practice the conversation. Then make new conversations with the problems in Exercise A.

WHAT ABOUT YOU?

GROUPS Have you returned anything to a store? Describe your experience.

Read a menu

Where do you usually eat breakfast, lunch, and dinner?
At home? In a restaurant?

○○○○○○ **MENUS**

A **Read the menu. What time is the café open?**

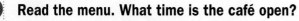
Healthy Café
Open 11:00 A.M. – 2:00 P.M.

Appetizers $3.50
Tomato soup
Chicken and rice soup
Green salad
Baked potato with cheese

Drinks $1.00
Coffee/Tea
Juice – Apple and Orange
Iced Tea
Milk

Entrees $5.00
Hamburger
Chicken sandwich
Fish sandwich

Desserts $2.50
Apple pie
Cheesecake
Ice cream

B ◀)) **Listen. What does the customer order for lunch?**
Write the items on the lines.

_____

_____

_____

_____

WHAT ABOUT YOU?

PAIRS Take turns. Say what you like on the menu.

LISTENING AND SPEAKING

Order from a menu

GET READY

Carmen is at the deli counter.
Guess. What is she asking Truda?

WATCH

A ▶ Watch the video. Was your guess correct?

B ▶ Watch the video again. Read the sentences. Circle the correct answers.

1. Carmen orders some food for _____.

    a. breakfast   **b.** lunch   **c.** dinner

2. There are _____ specials today.

    a. two   **b.** three   **c.** four

3. Carmen orders a medium container of _____.

    a. green salad   **b.** soup   **c.** fruit salad

4. Carmen is getting _____ to drink.

    a. tea   **b.** juice   **c.** milk

CONVERSATION

A ▶ Watch part of the video. Complete the conversation.

Truda: We have two specials today. Grilled _____ and broccoli,
and pasta with tomato sauce.
    ★

Carmen: They both sound good! I'll take a large container of pasta and sauce and

a medium container of _____ salad.
    ★★

Truda: Sure. We have fresh garlic bread, too.

Carmen: OK. I'll take some.

Truda: Here you go. Anything else?

Carmen: No, thanks.

> **Pronunciation Note**
>
> In conversation, the word *and*
> is usually short and quiet: "'n'."
> Link *and* to the word before it.
>
> ◀))) **Listen and repeat.**
>
> chicken‿an∅ broccoli
> pasta‿an∅ sauce

B ◀))) Listen and repeat.

C PAIRS Practice the conversation.

D PAIRS Practice the conversation again. Use different foods.

WHAT DO YOU THINK?

GROUPS Carmen orders takeout food because she is tired.
Do you order takeout food? Why?

LESSON 8

LISTENING AND SPEAKING

Accept an invitation

GET READY

Oscar invites Carmen to a party.

Guess. Why is he having a party?

WATCH

A **Watch the video. Was your guess correct?**

B **Watch the video again. Read the sentences. Circle *True* or *False*. Then correct the false sentences.**

1. Oscar needs to talk to Carmen about work.	True	False
2. Oscar invites Carmen to a birthday party.	True	False
3. Carmen is going to bring a dessert.	True	False
4. Wen is going to the party.	True	False
5. Oscar is going to have a special cake for Wen.	True	False

CONVERSATION

A **Watch part of the video. Complete the conversation.**

Oscar: We're going to have a party this Saturday evening.
______________________?
★

Carmen: ______________________! What's the party for?
★★

Oscar: We got the new apartment.

Carmen: Congratulations! What time does the party start?

Oscar: Five o'clock.

Pronunciation Note

When we talk to friends, we sometimes pronounce *going to* "gonna" when it comes before a verb.

Listen and repeat.

We're going to have a party.

I know what I'm going to make.

B **Listen and repeat.**

C PAIRS **Practice the conversation.**

D PAIRS **Practice the conversation again. Use different ways to extend and accept an invitation.**

WHAT DO YOU THINK?

PAIRS Oscar got the new apartment, so he's having a housewarming party. Carmen wants to bring a gift. What are some appropriate gift ideas?

I think a large candle is a nice gift . . .

9 Be going to

STUDY *Be going to*

Affirmative Statements			
I'm You're She's We're They're	**going to**	**buy**	clothes.
		see	a movie.
		have	a party.
It's	**going to**	**rain.**	

Negative Statements				
I'm You're She's We're They're	**not**	**going to**	**tell**	him.
It's	**not**	**going to**	**rain.**	

Grammar Note

I am = I'm	*We are = We're*
You are = You're	*They are = They're*
He is, She is = He's, She's	*It is = It's*

PRACTICE

A **Complete the sentences. Use *is* and *are*.**

1. It _'s not_____ going to rain tomorrow. (not)

2. Wen _____ going to get a promotion.

3. You _____ going to take your break later.

4. We _____ going to see the new movie tonight.

5. I _____ going to leave yet. (not)

B **Complete the sentences about this weekend. Use *be going to*.**

Carmen and her daughters ____*are going to go shopping*____.
　　　　　　　　　　　　　　　　1. go shopping

Oscar and Isabel _____ a party.
　　　　　　　　　　　　2. have

Saba _____ the house.
　　　　　　　3. clean

Wen and Jim _____ on Saturday.
　　　　　　　　　4. not / work

Truda _____ with her family.
　　　5. not / stay home

WHAT ABOUT YOU?

GROUP What are you going to do this weekend?

I'm going to visit my grandmother.

10 Give an opinion

STUDY THE MODEL

A **Read Truda's email to her friend. Why did Truda write this email?**

> **From:** Truda Mazur March 18, 2015 10:20 P.M.
>
> Hi, Donna,
>
> Congratulations on your new job. I'm so excited for you!
>
> I'm still at Fresh Foods. My boss, Jim, thinks I'm a good worker. Every day I try to learn new things. I'm going to take a management course on the weekend. Jim thinks I should apply to be a manager someday. He believes I have the skills to be a good manager.
>
> Enjoy your new job and let's talk soon!
>
> Truda

B **Read the Writing Tip. Read the email again. What does Jim think about Truda? Underline the sentences with *think* and *believe*.**

Writing Tip

Use words such as *think* and *believe* to write about **opinions** and **beliefs**.

BEFORE YOU WRITE

PAIRS Think about your skills. What are you good at? What do you believe you can do in the future? Share your opinions.

WRITE

Write about your skills and your future goal or goals. Study Truda's email and the Writing Tip.

∘∘∘∘ °°
GET READY

Do you like to try new things and have new experiences?

∘∘∘∘ °°
READ

◄))) **Listen and read the article. Where are people eating?**

Dining in the dark

LIVING

Imagine. You are sitting in a restaurant. The waiter puts your food in front of you. You can smell it. You can touch it. You can taste it. But you cannot see it. There are no lights or candles in the restaurant. All the windows and curtains are closed. No one can see their food. Everyone is in the dark.

The first "dark dining" restaurant opened in Switzerland in 1999. It was called *Blindkuh* or Blind Cow in English. People came to the restaurant to try a new way of eating. When people did not see their food, they gave more attention to the food's smell, taste, and feel. It was a new experience.

Today, cities from San Francisco, California, to Bangkok, Thailand, have dark-dining restaurants. How does it work? The restaurant is completely dark. You cannot see anything. You feel like you are blind. Your waiter helps you walk to your table. You cannot bring lighters, cell phones, or anything that can make light. The menu does not have many choices. You take your time and pay attention to your food. You talk about your food with your friends. You taste, feel, and smell the food in a new way.

What about you? Do you want to try dark dining? Or are you happy to keep the lights on?

∘∘∘∘ °°
AFTER YOU READ

Read the Reading Skill. Find the word **dark**. Look at the words and sentences around it. Can you guess what it means?

Reading Skill
If you don't know a word, look at **the words and sentences around it**. They can help you **guess** the meaning of the word.

WHAT DO YOU THINK?

PAIRS Talk about these senses: seeing, touching, tasting, hearing, and smelling. Which one do you think is most important? Why?

JOB-SEEKING SKILLS
Get hired

Sara *Today*
I'm waiting to hear about the job at Fresh Foods. I hope I get the job.

GET READY

Imagine. Sara's telephone rings. It's Fresh Foods. What do you think?
Did Sara get the job? How do you think she feels?

GET HIRED

A ◀ᴗ)) **Listen to the conversation. Sara is taking notes. Complete the notes.**

Job: _____

Schedule

Days: _____

Time: _____

Next Steps

Come to _____ for orientation

on _____ at _____ .

Bring _____ .

B ◀ᴗ)) **Listen again. Circle the correct answers.**

1. Sarah has a job orientation next _____.
   a. week   b. month

2. She got the _____ shift.
   a. morning   b. day

3. The appointment is at _____.
   a. 10:30 A.M.   b. 8:30 A.M.

4. She needs to bring _____ pieces of government identification with her.
   a. two   b. three

PUT YOUR IDEAS TO WORK

PAIRS Write notes about a job that you want. Use the information in Exercise A.
Give the notes to your partner. Role play a phone conversation between a
human resources representative and a job applicant. Then switch roles.

GRAMMAR

In this unit, you studied:

- Simple present: *Wh-* questions
- *Be going to*

See page 154 for your Grammar Review.

VOCABULARY See page 160 for the Unit 10 Vocabulary.

Vocabulary Learning Strategy: Label objects

A Write 10 words on Post-It notes or labels
and place them on the objects in your home.

jeans

B Choose 5 words from Exercise A. Write a sentence
with each word on a separate piece of paper.

SPELLING See page 160 for the Unit 10 Vocabulary.

CLASS Choose 10 words for a spelling test.

LISTENING PLUS

A Watch each video. Write the story of Carmen's day on a separate piece of paper.

> *Carmen calls her mother. They make plans to take Carmen's*
> *daughters shopping for clothes.*

B **PAIRS** Review the conversation in Lesson 5 (see page 136).
Role play the conversation for the class.

NOW I CAN

PAIRS See page 131 for the Unit 10 Goals. Check ☑ the things you can do.
Underline the things you want to study more. Tell your partner.

> I can _____. I need more practice with _____.

GRAMMAR REVIEW

SIMPLE PRESENT WITH *BE* AND POSSESSIVE ADJECTIVES

Complete the email from Truda's husband, Stefan. Use words from the box. If the word starts a sentence, capitalize the first letter. Use some words more than once.

> The first word in a sentence needs to be capitalized.

| are | her | his | I'm | is | it's | our | she's | their |

Truda has a new job. (1) __She's__ a deli associate at Fresh Foods. Fresh Foods

(2) _____ on Duke Street. (3) _____ a big supermarket. The workers

(4) _____ busy.

Truda likes (5) _____ boss. (6) _____ name is Jim. She likes (7) _____

coworker, Joe, too. Truda (8) _____ friends with Carmen. Carmen (9) _____

a cashier. Truda and Carmen like (10) _____ jobs.

When Truda (11) _____ at work, (12) _____ children (13) _____ with a

babysitter. The babysitter (14) _____ really nice.

Truda (15) _____ very happy. (16) _____ really happy, too.

SINGULAR AND PLURAL NOUNS

Look at the pictures. Complete the sentences.

1. The three ___men___ are coworkers.

2. Truda has two _____.

3. The _____ is under the counter.

4. Carmen and I are _____.

5. The _____ is in the back.

6. Where are the _____?

GRAMMAR REVIEW

BE: SIMPLE PRESENT NEGATIVE STATEMENTS

Write two negative statements with each word from the box.

> upset   busy   ~~married~~   tired   hungry   open

1. Carmen   *Carmen is not married.*   *She's not married.*

2. You   _____   _____

3. I   _____   _____

4. We   _____   _____

5. Fresh Foods   _____   _____

6. Joe and Wen   _____   _____

BE: SIMPLE PRESENT YES / NO QUESTIONS

**Look at each picture and adjective. Write a yes / no question.
Then write a short affirmative or negative answer.**

1.
(she / stressed)   *Is she stressed?*   *Yes, she is.*

2.
(he / tall)   _____   _____

3.
(they / happy)   _____   _____

4.
(they / tired)   _____   _____

5.
(she / healthy)   _____   _____

THIS, THAT, THESE, THOSE

Complete the conversations. Use *this*, *that*, *these*, or *those*.

1. **Customer:** _____This_____ change is not correct.

   Carmen: I'm so sorry!

2. **Customer:** Can you do a price check on _____?

   Carmen: Sure.

3. **Customer:** How much are the red onions over there?

   Oscar: _____ onions are $3.99 a pound.

4. **Oscar:** Can you help me unload _____ boxes?

   Wen: Yes. Where do you want them?

SIMPLE PRESENT: STATEMENTS

Complete the sentences in Truda's email. Use the simple present.

○○○

Dear Maria,

Thank you so much for babysitting! Here is the kids' schedule:

Elena and Boris _need_ a snack at around 10:00. Elena _____
         1. need   2. not/like

bananas. Boris _____ all kinds of fruit. Then they _____
              3. like   4. have

lunch around twelve o'clock. Sometimes they _____ all of their food.
                                                  5. not/eat

That's OK! After lunch, they _____ naps.
                                    6. take

I _____ work at 5:00. I can be home by 5:30.
     7. finish

See you tomorrow morning!

Truda

BE SIMPLE PRESENT QUESTIONS WITH *WHERE*

Look at the picture. Complete the conversation between Saba and Ana, a new employee. Use the simple present. Use *Where* if necessary.

1. **Ana:** Where is the deli counter?
   Saba: It's in the back of the store, on the right.

2. **Ana:** Where are the frozen foods?
   Saba: _____

3. **Ana:** _____
   Saba: It's at the end of Aisle 3.

4. **Ana:** Where is the bakery?
   Saba: _____

5. **Ana:** _____
   Saba: They're in the back of the store, on the left.

6. **Ana:** Where is the dairy section?
   Saba: _____

DESCRIPTIVE ADJECTIVES

Complete each sentence with a word from each box.

busy friendly salty yellow ~~young~~	~~children~~ employee foods onions store

1. Truda is married. She has two _____young_____ _____children_____.
   They go to a babysitter while Truda is at work.

2. Jim wants to be healthy. He doesn't eat _____ _____.

3. Fresh Foods has many customers. It is a _____ _____.

4. Carmen loves to make her grandmother's spicy bean soup.
   She needs two _____ _____ to make the soup.

5. Wen loves people and enjoys helping customers.
   He is a _____ _____.

SIMPLE PRESENT *YES / NO* QUESTIONS: *HAVE, HURT*

Complete the conversation between Jim and Truda. Use the simple present.

Jim: You don't look well. What's the matter?

Truda: I feel sick.

Jim: *Does your head hurt?*
 <u>1. your / head / hurt</u>

Truda: _____.
 2. yes

Jim: Oh, dear. _____?
 3. your / throat / hurt

Truda: _____.
 4. no

Jim: Well, that's good. _____?
 5. have / fever

Truda: _____.
 6. no

Jim: I'm glad to hear it. Two of Oscar's workers are out sick.

Truda: Oh no! _____?
 7. have / flu

Jim: I'm not sure.

Truda: _____
 8. their / stomachs / hurt

Jim: _____
 9. yes

Truda: I hope they feel better soon!

BE: SIMPLE PRESENT QUESTIONS WITH *WHAT*

Complete the email from Dora. Use *is* or *are*.

Happy Birthday, Carmen! We need to celebrate! Let's go out for dinner. What

(1) *are* your days off next week? Let's have lunch or dinner together. What

(2) _____ the best time for you?

Also, what (3) _____ the girls up to? Maybe they can come, too. What

(4) _____ their after-school schedule?

You should choose the restaurant. What (5) _____ your favorite restaurant

these days? Do you still like Vinny's Pasta and Pizza? We can go anywhere.

Can't wait to see you!

IMPERATIVES

**Complete the imperative sentences. Use the verbs from the box.
Use the negative if necessary.**

bring   call   do   ~~drive~~   eat   take

1. _____Don't_____ _____drive_____ on Center Street. There is an accident.

2. _____ to the store, please. We need some milk.

3. _____ between 9 A.M. and 5 P.M. to make an appointment.

4. _____ _____ at that restaurant. It's terrible!

5. _____ your homework now!

6. _____ an ID with you.

SHOULD / SHOULDN'T

**Wen gives his friend Dennis advice for his new job.
Complete the email. Use *should* or *shouldn't* and the verbs.**

It's great that you have a new job! You _____should go_____ at least 15
                                            1. go
minutes early the first day. You _____ late. Also, you
                                        2. not / be
_____ your ID because you have to fill out many forms.
      3. bring
You _____ yourself to your coworkers and talk to them,
          4. introduce
but you _____ them personal questions. You also
              5. not / ask
_____ too long a lunch break.
      6. not / take

Good luck on your first day! —Wen

POSSESSIVE NOUNS

Read the email from Isabel to her cousin, Olivia. Add apostrophes (') to show possession.

Hi, Olivia.

We're really happy about our new apartment. It's close to my <u>parents' apartment</u>,
                                                                        1.
but it's a little far from <u>Oscars job</u>. We like the <u>childrens school</u>. <u>Sofias teacher</u> is
                                2.   3.   4.
really good. <u>Alexs teacher</u> is very helpful. Our <u>neighbors children</u> go to the same
                     5.   6.
school. They're very friendly.

Take care and talk soon!

Isabel

THERE IS / THERE ARE STATEMENTS

**Look at the pictures of apartments Oscar saw. Complete the sentences.
Use *there is, there isn't, there are,* or *there aren't*.**

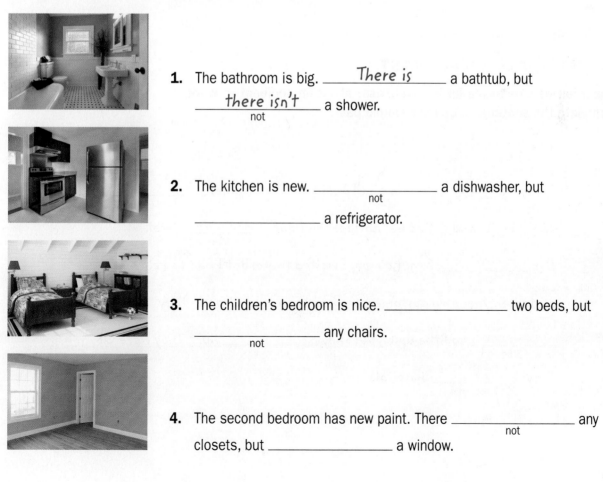

1. The bathroom is big. _____*There is*_____ a bathtub, but
   _____*there isn't*_____ a shower.
                    not

2. The kitchen is new. _____ a dishwasher, but
                             not
   _____ a refrigerator.

3. The children's bedroom is nice. _____ two beds, but
   _____ any chairs.
        not

4. The second bedroom has new paint. There _____ any
                                                    not
   closets, but _____ a window.

CAN / CAN'T

What can the Fresh Foods employees do? Write questions and answers. Use *can* or *can't*.

1. (Carmen / use / a scanner)

    A: _Can Carmen use a scanner?_

    B: Yes, _she can._

2. (Wen and Joe / prepare / deli foods)

    A: _____

    B: No, _____

3. (Oscar / supervise / employees)

    A: _____

    B: Yes, _____

4. (Truda and Jim / make / sandwiches)

    A: _____

    B: Yes, _____

5. (Saba / unload / produce)

    A: _____

    B: No, _____

BE, HAVE, GO: SIMPLE PAST

**Oscar leaves a message for his supervisor about an accident at work.
Complete the sentences. Use the simple past.**

Hi Alan,

Today we _had_ a small accident. A customer _____
⟶ 1. have   2. not / be

very careful and spilled her coffee. The floor _____ wet.
3. be

Joe _____ to get a mop. I waited there, but I had to help a
4. go

customer. Then two customers walked there and slipped. They

_____ a little upset, but they _____ hurt. They were OK.
5. be   6. not / be

They _____ hospital.
7. not / go

PRESENT CONTINUOUS: STATEMENTS

What is happening at Fresh Foods right now? Complete the sentences.
Use the present continuous.

1. Carmen _____*is scanning*_____ an item.
_{scan}

2. A customer _____ meat at the deli.
_{order}

3. Oscar and Wen _____ in the produce section.
_{talk}

4. Saba _____ a customer.
_{help}

5. Carmen and Wen _____ lunch together.
_{eat}

OBJECT PRONOUNS

Oscar is talking to his coworkers. Complete the sentences.
Use the object pronouns from the box.

| her   him   it   me   ~~them~~   us |

1. "Do you see those boxes? Please give ____*them*____ to Wen."

2. "Joe needs a hand. Help _____ unload the produce, please."

3. "Wen and I have our break at noon. Can you eat lunch with _____?"

4. "Saba has the forms. Please see _____."

5. "I need a signature on your timesheet. Please sign _____."

6. "I want to talk to you. Can you stop by my office and see _____?"

SIMPLE PRESENT: *WH-* QUESTIONS

**Marta asks her sister Carmen to come to Oscar's housewarming party.
Complete the conversation. Write *wh-* questions in the simple present.**

Carmen: Marta, do you want to come to Oscar's party? It's on Saturday.

Marta: Sure. <u>When</u> <u>does</u> the party start?

           1.

Carmen: It starts at 3 P.M.

Marta: _____ _____ Oscar live?

         2.

Carmen: He lives in Springfield.

Marta: OK. _____ _____ you want to leave for the party?

         3.

Carmen: Let's leave at 2:30 P.M.

Marta: Sounds good.

Carmen: Oh . . . _____ _____ I need to bring?

         4.

Marta: You don't need to bring anything.

Carmen: And _____ _____ I need to wear? Is it a fancy party?

         5.

Marta: No! You can wear jeans.

FUTURE WITH *BE GOING TO*

**Read Carmen's email to her friend Jennifer. Complete the sentences.
Use *be going to* and the verbs.**

It <u>is going to be</u> a fun weekend! I _____ to a party at my

  1. be   2. go

coworker's new apartment. We _____ a cake for another coworker

                             3. have

who got a promotion. He doesn't know about the cake. He _____ so

                             4. be

surprised! The girls and I _____ fruit salad. My sister

                    5. bring

_____ with us. What fun!

  6. come

Hope you have a good weekend, too!

GRAMMAR REFERENCES

UNIT 1 LESSON 5, page 10

Spelling rules for plural count nouns

Add **-s** to most nouns.

*book—book**s***

Add **-es** to nouns that end in **-ch**, **-s**, **-sh**, **-x**, or a consonant + **o**.

*watch—watch**es***   *box—box**es***
*guess—guess**es***   *potato—potato**es***
*dish—dish**es***

Change **y** to **i** and add **-es** to nouns that end in a consonant + **y**.

*baby—bab**ies***   *city—cit**ies***

Change **f** to **v** and add **-s** to nouns that end in **-fe**.

*knife—kni**ves***   *wife—wi**ves***

Change **f** to **v** and add **-es** to nouns that end in **-f**.

*loaf—loa**ves***   *shelf—shel**ves***

Some plural nouns are irregular.

child	**children**
man	**men**
woman	**women**
person	**people**
foot	**feet**
tooth	**teeth**

UNIT 3, LESSON 7, page 40

Spelling rules for simple present: Third person singular (*he*, *she*, *it*)

Add **-s** for most verbs.

*work—work**s***   *run—run**s***

Add **-es** for words that end in **-ch**, **-s**, **-sh**, **-x**, or **-z**.

*watch—watch**es***   *relax—relax**es***

Change **y** to **i** and add **-es** when the base form ends in a consonant + **y**.

*study—stud**ies***

Add **-s** when the base form ends in a vowel + **y**.

*play—play**s***   *enjoy—enjoy**s***

Some verbs have **irregular forms**.

*do—**does***   *have—**has***   *go—**goes***

UNIT 9, LESSON 3, page 120

Spelling rules for the present continuous

Add **-ing** to the base form of most verbs.

*cook—cook**ing***   *eat—eat**ing***

For verbs that end in **e**, drop the final **e** and add **-ing**.

*take—tak**ing***   *make—mak**ing***

For one-syllable verbs that end in a consonant, a vowel, and a consonant, double the final consonant and add **-ing**. Do not double the final consonant if it is a **w**, **x**, or **y**.

*get—gett**ing***   *play—play**ing***

WORD LIST

WELCOME UNIT

listen
look at
open

point to
put away
read

a student identification
    card
take out

write

UNIT 1

Lesson 1
a customer
an employee
introduce
shake hands
a shopping cart

Lesson 2
a baker
the bakery
a butcher
a dairy associate
the dairy department
the deli
a deli worker
the meat department
a produce associate
the produce department

Lesson 4
above
aprons
a fork

gloves
a knife
on
paper towels
a spoon
under

Lesson 6
at the back
at the front
bakery
checkout
customer service
dairy section
deli counter
entrance
frozen foods
international section
next to
on the left
on the right
produce section
restrooms

Lesson 7
brother
children
daughter
excellent
father
fine
grandfather
grandmother
great
husband
mother
parents
sister
son
That's great!
wife

Lesson 9
one
two
three
four

five
six
seven
eight
nine
area code
extension

Lesson 11
floor
lucky
married

Job-Seeking Skills
a full-time job
an indoor job
an outdoor job
a part-time job
transportation

UNIT 2

Lesson 1
all right
happy
OK
sick
stressed
upset

Lesson 3
after lunch
blond hair
hungry
short
tall
thin
tomorrow

Lesson 5
bills
cash
a check

coins
a credit card

Lesson 6
apples
a bag
bananas
a bunch
a carrot
onions
oranges
peppers
a pineapple
potatoes
a pound
tomatoes

Lesson 7
buy one, get one free
a coupon
the price

a receipt
a savings card
swipe your card
two for $5

Lesson 8
change
an error
I apologize
I made a mistake
a problem
tax
total

Lesson 9
date
items
payment
potatoes
subtotal

Lesson 11
go shopping
make a budget
save money
spend money
talk about something
think about something

Job-Seeking Skills
come to work on time
job skills
personality traits
use a cash register
use a computer
work with machines
work with people

WORD LIST

UNIT 3

Lesson 1
an accident
Have a good day.
a highway
See you later.
Talk to you later.
traffic

Lesson 2
do not enter
a lane
merge left
pedestrian crossing
no left turn sign
no right turn sign
no U-turn
speed limit
a stop sign
a traffic light
yield

Lesson 3
boxes
broccoli
carry
a melon
no problem
a shopping basket
sure
unpack

Lesson 5
a flyer
fruits
vegetables

Lesson 6
chili peppers
fish
garlic
green

I'd like some
I'm looking for
red
spicy
sweet
yellow

Lesson 8
A.M.
It's one o'clock.
It's 1:15.
It's 1:30.
P.M.
a quarter to two

Lesson 9
early
a garage
late

Lesson 11
afraid
charge
cold
a parking space
plug in
pollution
wet

Job-Seeking Skills
apply
customer service
necessary
a positive attitude

UNIT 4

Lesson 1
deodorant
paper towels
razor blades
shampoo
soap
tissues
toothpaste

Lesson 3
arm
back
chest
elbow
feet/foot
hand
leg
shoulder
stomach

Lesson 4
fall
find
get hurt
have an accident
look for
a mop
slip
spill
a warning sign
a wet floor

Lesson 5
beans
cilantro
delicious
large
medium
a recipe

small
soup
wonderful

Lesson 7
afternoon
evening
month
morning
night
a weekday
the weekend

Lesson 8
day off
day shift
night shift

Lesson 9
a menu
the movies
a party

Lesson 10
blood pressure
gain weight
memory

Job-Seeking Skills
experience required—
    exp req
full-time—FT
Monday to Friday—M–F
part-time—PT
reference—ref
weekends—wknds

WORD LIST

UNIT 5

Lesson 1
It's cloudy.
It's hot.
It's raining.
It's snowing.
It's sunny.
It's windy.
seasons

Lesson 2
an adhesive bandage
bleed
chest
a cough
a fever

the flu
a headache
a stomachache

Lesson 4
days
a month
a week
a year

Lesson 6
appointment
look up
opening
a patient
system

Lesson 7
cancel
confirm
date
a doctor
a patient
time

Lesson 8
birthdate
contact numbers
computer
current address

Lesson 10
a clinic
a drugstore
expensive
a sore throat

Lesson 11
paychecks

Job-Seeking Skills
availability
immediately
interested in
overtime
personal information
required

UNIT 6

Lesson 1
a driver's license
forms of ID
a health insurance card
an identification card
a passport
a Social Security card

Lesson 3
arrival
a sign-in sheet

Lesson 4
an examining table
a flashlight
hold out your arm
look straight ahead
make a fist

open your mouth and
   say "ahh"
sit on the table
a stethoscope
take a deep breath
a waiting room

Lesson 5
chills
cough medicine
exhausted
a thermometer
throat

Lesson 6
drowsy
liquid
a pharmacist

sleepy
tablets
tired

Lesson 7
a backache
capsules
dosage
an expiration date
a label
a pain reliever
a toothache
a warning

Lesson 8
rest
tea
worried

Lesson 10
dangerous
sneezing
spices

Job-Seeking Skills
graduate
highest level of
   education
per hour
reason for leaving
recent
a supervisor
the U.S. military
work history

WORD LIST

UNIT 7

Lesson 1
an apartment
a condominium
a house
painters

Lesson 2
Avenue—Ave.
Boulevard—Blvd.
Drive—Dr.
Road—Rd.
Street—St.

Lesson 3
bathroom—BA
bedroom—BR
dining room—DR
kitchen—K

living room—LR
utilities—util.
washer and dryer—W/D

Lesson 4
expensive
friendly
quiet

Lesson 6
a compass
directions
exit
GPS
left
right
straight

Lesson 7
across from
between
next to

Lesson 8
a bathtub
a closet
a dishwasher
a refrigerator
a shower
a stove
a window

Lesson 11
a couch
a hotel
surf
travel

Job-Seeking Skills
get a good night's sleep
make eye contact
nervous
put your hands in
   your lap
shake hands
sit up straight
smile
wear clean and neat
   clothes

UNIT 8

Lesson 1
arrive
a bus
miss
a subway

Lesson 2
operate a forklift
a promotion
stock
take inventory

Lesson 4
a baseball game
a concert
a gym
a movie
a museum
a party
a restaurant

Lesson 6
a bank
community
country
a family
a fire station
a gas station
home
a hospital
a library
a police station
a post office
world

Lesson 7
a bus stop
an express bus
a fare card
get off
get on

a metro station
a stop
transportation
weekday service

Lesson 8
Apartment—Apt.
Avenue—Ave.
Boulevard—Blvd.
Road—Rd.
Street—St.

Lesson 9
avocadoes
celery
corn
cucumbers
lettuce
a pound

special
spinach

Lesson 10
crowded
a dessert
noisy
order
recommend

Job-Seeking Skills
evening shift
an interview
legally work

WORD LIST

UNIT 9

Lesson 1
celebrate
a custodian
fantastic
a hospital
a hotel

Lesson 2
cracked
a faucet
fix
a leak
a lock
moldy
a sink
stuck
a toilet
water damage

Lesson 4
an emergency contact
forms
a paycheck
a pay stub

Lesson 5
deductions
an employee
hours
federal taxes
medical insurance
net pay
pay date
a pay period
pay rate
regular hours
SSN

state income tax
total pay
overtime

Lesson 6
an emergency contact
   form
relationship

Lesson 7
an ambulance
chest pains
choking
paramedics
unconscious

Lesson 9
authorized
be careful

caution
fire
gloves
personnel
trespassing
wash your hands
watch your step

Lesson 11
911
dangerous
an emergency
firefighters
a flat tire
police
a robbery
a serious medical
   problem

UNIT 10

Lesson 1
a belt
a dress
a coat
jeans
pajamas
sandals
shorts
socks

Lesson 3
shoes
a skirt
a sweater
pants
a T-shirt
underwear

Lesson 4
batteries
dish towels

a gift card
exchange
an item
pantyhose
a receipt
return
store credit

Lesson 5
short
tight
wrong color

Lesson 6
an appetizer
apple pie
a café
cheese
cheesecake
drinks
entrees

fish
grilled chicken
a hamburger
a sandwich

Lesson 7
carrot salad
containers
fruit salad
garlic
grilled shrimp
spinach salad
with tomato sauce

Lesson 8
a cake
a party
a surprise

Lesson 11
blind
a candle
dark
dine
experience
a lighter
lights
smell
taste
touch

Job-Seeking Skills
confident
a human resources
   representative
identification

Fedmart
Employment Application

Personal Information

Name _____ Phone # _____

Street _____ City _____ State ____ Zip Code _____

When can you begin to work? _____

Are you interested in full-time? _____ Part-time? _____

Can you work overtime? Yes _____ No_____

	Sunday	Monday	Tuesday	Wednesday	Thursday	Friday	Saturday
From							
To							

Are you legally able to work in the U.S.? Yes _____ No _____

Most Recent Education

School Name _____ Address _____

City _____ State ____ Zip Code _____ Phone Number _____

Courses _____

Highest Level of Education Completed _____

Did you graduate from high school? Yes _____ No _____ GED Diploma _____

Work History (list your most recent jobs)

1. Company _____ Phone # _____

   Street _____ City _____ State ____ Zip Code _____

   Job _____ Supervisor _____

   Dates Worked _____ Salary _____

   Reason for Leaving _____

2. Company _____ Phone # _____

   Street _____ City _____ State ____ Zip Code _____

   Job _____ Supervisor _____

   Dates Worked _____ Salary _____

   Reason for Leaving _____

Military History

Have you served in the U.S. military? Yes _____ No _____

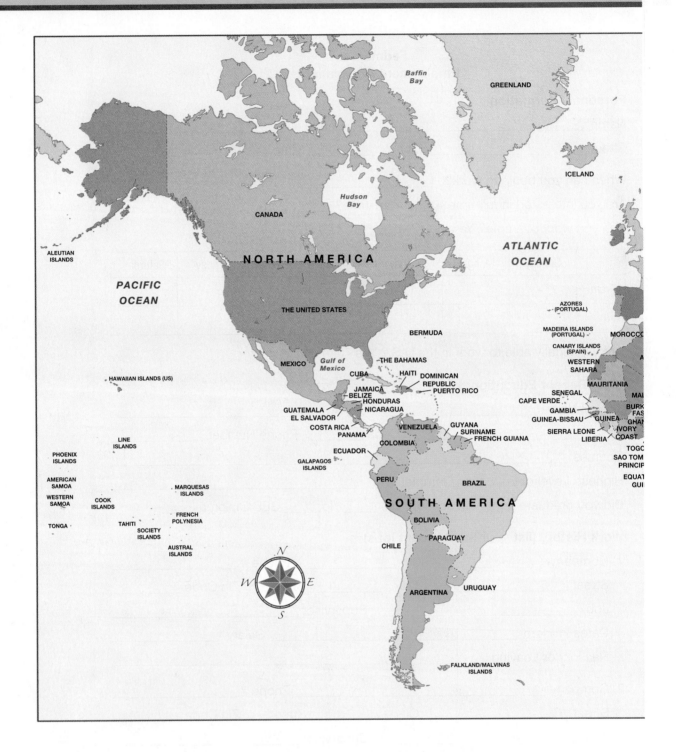

MAPS

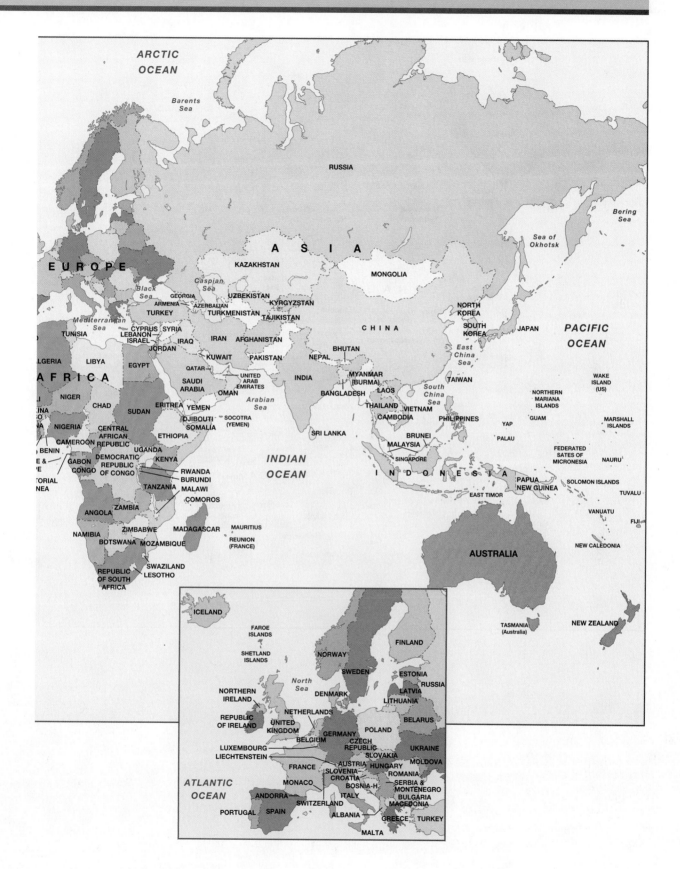

CREDITS

PHOTOS

Cover Photos: Matthew Howe, Photographer. Student Book: All original photography by Matthew Howe, Photographer. Page 2 Andriianov/Fotolia; p. 17 diego cervo/Fotolia; p. 24 ($1) 2happy/Shutterstock, ($5) Voronin76/Shutterstock, ($10) Garsya/Shutterstock, ($20) Steve Stock/Alamy, (coins) usmint. gov; p. 31 diego cervo/Fotolia; p. 38 (top left) Oleksiy Ilyashenko/Fotolia, (top right) msk.nina/Fotolia, (middle left) Dionisvera/Fotolia, (middle right) Ruslan Kuzmenkov/Shutterstock, (bottom left) Sergii Moscaliuk/Fotolia, (bottom right) Anna Kucherova/Fotolia; p. 45 diego cervo/Fotolia; p. 57 rubberball/ Glow Images; p. 59 diego cervo/Fotolia; p. 71 AP Images/NATI HARNIK; p. 73 diego cervo/ Fotolia; p. 85 senk/Shutterstock; p. 87 diego cervo/Fotolia; p. 91 PHILETDOM/Fotolia; p. 92 GP/ Fotolia; p. 98 melikosan/Shutterstock; p. 100 StockLite/Shutterstock; p. 101 (top) diego cervo/ Fotolia, (bottom) goodluz/Fotolia; p. 109 (a) David R. Frazier Photolibrary, Inc./Alamy, (b) Giuseppe Porzani/Fotolia, (c) Tyler Olson/Fotolia, (d) VILevi/Shutterstock, (e) DavidPinoPhotography/ Shutterstock, (f) GlowImages/Alamy, (g) Denise Kappa/Shutterstock, (h) Ryan McVay/Getty Images; p. 113 T-Design/Shutterstock; p. 115 diego cervo/Fotolia; p. 126 (1) ninsiri/Shutterstock, (2) iofoto/ Shutterstock, (3) Neale Cousland/Shutterstock, (4) steliangagiu/Shutterstock, (5) Thomas Pajot/ Fotolia, (6) Lana Sundman/Alamy; p. 128 Cartoonresource/Shutterstock; p. 129 diego cervo/ Fotolia; p. 137 (top left) Jacek Chabraszewski/Fotolia, (top right) karandaev/Fotolia, (bottom left) ExQuisine/Fotolia, (bottom right) Blinztree/Fotolia; p. 143 diego cervo/Fotolia; p. 145 (1) lawcain/ Fotolia, (2) Warren Goldswain/Fotolia, (3) sparkia/Fotolia, (4) nexusseven/Fotolia, (5) koya79/Fotolia, (6) Ben Chams/Fotolia; p. 146 (1) Karramba Production/Fotolia, (2) Monart Design/Fotolia, (3) Andres Rodriguez/Fotolia, (4) auremar/Fotolia (5) Peter Atkins/Fotolia; p. 151 (1) Iriana Shiyan/Fotolia, (2) Iriana Shiyan/Fotolia, (3) poligonchik/Fotolia, (4) ArenaCreative/Fotolia.

ILLUSTRATIONS

ElectraGraphics, Inc., pp. 16, 44, 142, 162–164; Brian Hughes, 134; Rob Schuster, pp. 25, 35, 96; Gary Torrisi, p. 114; TSI Graphics, pp. 11, 41; TSI Graphics/John Kurtz, pp. 37, 50; Anna Veltfort, pp. 2, 3, 41, 136.